# TEN
# LIES
# ABOUT
# GOD

# TEN
# LIES
# ABOUT
# GOD

## AND HOW YOU
## MAY ALREADY
## BE DECEIVED

## ERWIN W. LUTZER

W PUBLISHING GROUP™

www.wpublishinggroup.com

*A Division of Thomas Nelson, Inc.*
*www.ThomasNelson.com*

Published by W Publishing Group, a Division of Thomas Nelson, Inc., P. O. Box 141000, Nashville, Tennessee 37214.

Unless otherwise noted, Scripture quotations are from the *Holy Bible, New International Version* Copyright © 1973, 1978, 1984 International Bible Society. Used by permission of Zondervan Bible Publishers.

Scriptures noted NASB are from the *New American Standard Bible,* copyright © 1960, 1962, 1963, 1968, 1971, 1972, 1973, 1975, 1977 by The Lockman Foundation and are used by permission.

Scriptures noted NLT are from the *Holy Bible,* New Living Translation, copyright © 1996. Used by permission of Tyndale House Publishers, Inc., Wheaton, Illinois 60189. All rights reserved.

Scriptures noted KJV are from the King James Version of the Bible.

### Library of Congress-in-Publication Data

Lutzer, Erwin W.
Ten lies about God : and how you may already be deceived / Erwin W. Lutzer.
p. cm.
Includes bibliographical references.
ISBN 0-8499-1627-5 (hardcover)
ISBN 0-8499-4332-9 (trade paper)
1. God. I. Title.
BT102 .L88 2000
231—dc21                                                                00-033386

*Printed in the United States of America*

2 3 4 5 6 7 8 9 PHX 05 04 03 02

# Contents

To the God whose grace saved me when I was a child,
and whose power, wisdom, and mystery are my delight.
"Great is the LORD and most worthy of praise;
his greatness no one can fathom."
(Ps. 145:3)

# Preface:
## From My Heart to Yours

WHEN A COALITION of armies outnumbered King Jehoshaphat, he knew that his hope had to be in God alone. In desperation he prayed, "O our God, will you not judge them? For we have no power to face this vast army that is attacking us. We do not know what to do, *but our eyes are upon you*" (2 Chron. 20:12, emphasis mine). He knew that our greatest need is always to see God. The clearer our vision of Him, the more compelling our motivation to trust, obedience, and worship. A. W. Tozer was right when he said that what we believe about God is the most important thing about us.

But in what God shall we believe?

Although opinion polls tell us that 92 percent of Americans believe in God, the God of the Bible is not who they have in mind. According to journalist Chris Stamper, that deity "looks less and less like the one true God and more and more like the star of a do-it-yourself gospel pulled off a tray at the postmodern cafeteria."[1] This generation is through with a belief in a transcendent deity who could actually mess with our lives, rearrange our priorities, and force us to deal with that horrid concept, *sin*.

Our generation chooses instead to meet its spiritual needs by shopping for a faith that has fragments of Christianity mixed with Scientology, Buddhism, and any number of notions derived from "personal experience." Thus, although an overwhelming number of people will continue to say they believe in God, their conception of

God will be as diverse as the items in a shopping mall. Nietzsche was right: once God was declared dead, a "rain of gods" followed, with everyone worshiping his/her deity of choice.

In wider academic circles, we must also grapple with post-modernism, which claims that the whole idea of God is a social construct. No outside reality fixes the notion of God, it is said, but rather an individual or group of individuals decides it for themselves. In fact, there is no truth, religious or otherwise, that must be discovered; it must simply be "manufactured." Contemporary society discounts any claims to objective reason, declaring instead: "All that exists is what is in my mind, and my ideas are 'true' *simply because I think them.*"

These trends are understandable given our cultural drift; what is most lamentable is that such skewed notions of God also exist within the professing church. The grand vision of God given to us by the writers of Scripture has, to a great extent, been lost. What we have in its place is an emphasis on "felt needs" and "health and wealth." Worse, some who still want to be known as evangelicals deny that God knows the future, or that we must be saved only through faith in Christ. Many churchgoers derive their understanding of God as much from popular culture as from the Scriptures. They do not reject Christianity outright but refine it to fit in with the pluralism of today's "feel good" religion.

"In short," writes Os Guinness, "a sickness of our age is that we have fit bodies but flaccid minds and vacant souls. So, like a drowsy napper who falls off to sleep after a meal and is reluctant to rouse himself to answer the telephone, we find ourselves disinclined to heed the challenge to rise above our age."[2] If the Christian church could be aroused to heed the voice of God, quite possibly our entire indulgent culture might rouse itself and take a second look at its moral and spiritual malaise. But it must begin with individuals like ourselves who are willing to return to the God of the Scriptures and not be coopted by what C. S. Lewis called "Christianity and water," the view that says there is a good God in heaven, so we need not be concerned with difficult doctrines such as sin, hell, and redemption.

Again, the lies I expose in this book are rampant not only in popular culture, but also within the professing church. And while I have discerned these deceptions, obviously neither I nor any other writer has said the last word about God. This study has in fact humbled me, for the more I know about Him, the more I realize there is yet to know. I have become profoundly impressed with the repeated observation of Scripture that His ways are unfathomable. To probe the character of God to the extent we mortals can is surely the highest pursuit of the mind and heart. I've been on a journey, and I hope you will join me.

I have written this book with three deeply held convictions.

First, *we must derive our knowledge of God from the Bible alone, and not from personal preferences or experiences.* Of course, I do not think it is possible for us to entirely extricate ourselves from cultural influences, but as much as possible we must ask not what we *want* the Bible to say, but what the Bible does say. We shall soon discover that the God of the Bible differs sharply from competing deities. This God stands apart from the most intriguing idols.

Like all of us, I face the danger of idolatry, that is, the temptation to manufacture a god based on my own inclinations and experience. Social scientists tell us there is compelling evidence that each culture creates its own gods; in fact, such gods are often indistinguishable from the culture itself. Agricultural peoples develop gods of the sun and rain; ocean people worship the god of the sea and the moon. And we Americans, obsessed with consumerism and pleasure, have created a god who is tolerant of our lifestyles, lets us be in charge, and serves mainly to help us fulfill our potential. He is a god "just for us."

No one, I believe, would dare create the idea of the holy, transcendent God of the Bible. This sovereign One probes our most hidden thoughts, tells us that we must repent, and commands worship that ends all thoughts of personal self-aggrandizement. This God, as we shall see in the chapters that follow, has been revealed from heaven. Our task is to understand Him as He has chosen to reveal Himself, not as we think He ought to be.

My second conviction is that *the clearer we see God, the clearer we shall see ourselves.* Calvin was right when he said that no man can know himself unless he first knows God. In the presence of the Almighty, the yardstick by which we measure our own goodness is finally revealed. Consequently we shall quickly confess, as have the saints before us, "Woe to me! . . . I am ruined! For I am a man of unclean lips, and I live among a people of unclean lips, and my eyes have seen the King, the LORD Almighty" (Isa. 6:5). Thankfully, God does not leave us "ruined" but extends the healing of His loving mercy and grace.

Armed with this knowledge of who we are, we will be better fitted to order our lives according to eternal values. The restlessness within will give way to the peace of knowing that at last we have discovered the reason for which we were created. Our pursuit of God will profoundly affect every aspect of our lives. We will face life, even tragedies, with the faith of Jehoshaphat who confessed, "Our eyes are upon You."

Third, *the better we know God, the more fervently we shall worship Him.* When Job learned that his ten children were killed in a windstorm, he turned to God and worshiped. Keep in mind that at this point in his spiritual journey, he had no idea why this happened. Yet we read:

> At this, Job got up and tore his robe and shaved his head. Then he fell
> to the ground in worship and said:
>
> "Naked I came from my mother's womb,
>     and naked I will depart.
> The LORD gave and the LORD has taken away;
>     may the name of the LORD be praised."
>
> (Job 1:20–21)

Job learned to worship God even without explanations. Without being able to probe God's mind, without being privy to the fine print of the Almighty's hidden purposes, Job knew that his place was on the ground before the mysterious God in whom he had come to trust.

In this book I make no pretense of answering all of our questions about God. In fact, I shall raise issues that perhaps some readers have never pondered before. But to the extent that we see God in His glory and sovereignty, we *must* worship! I agree with John Stott, "There is something fundamentally flawed about a purely academic interest in God. God is not an appropriate object for cool, critical, detached, scientific observation and evaluation. No, the true knowledge of God will always lead to worship. . . . Our place is on our faces before him in adoration."[3]

Yes, our desire is to be "on our faces before him in adoration." Thus at the end of each chapter I have included a personal response that I hope will motivate you to express your devotion to Him. I invite you to join in the glad sacrifice of worship and awe. I pray that you shall be changed even as I have been by contemplating our great and merciful God.

Join me on a journey designed to probe the mysteries of the Almighty, a journey that will motivate us to take our place with Job, faces to the ground, hearts raised in worship.

**LIE 1**

# God Is Whatever We Want Him to Be

ART LINKLETTER SAW A SMALL BOY scrawling wildly on a sheet of paper. "What are you drawing?" Linkletter asked.

"I'm drawing a picture of God."

"You can't do that, because nobody knows what God looks like."

"They will when I'm finished," the boy confidently replied.

What *does* God look like? Can we draw our own portrait of Him?

Whether we want to admit it or not, we are born to seek meaning, made to hunger for the spiritual; and behind those cravings is our search for God. The protagonist in a Carly Simon song traced his own spiritual journey from the halls of Cambridge to life in the country only to conclude:

> Now you run a bookstore
> And you have taken on a wife
> And wear patches on your elbows
> And you live an easy life.
> But are you finally satisfied?
> Is it what you were lookin' for?
> Or does it sneak up on you
> That there might be something more?[1]

Yes, we all hope for "something more." And throughout the ages, some of the greatest minds have believed that humankind could experience

1

"something more" only by finding God: "The soul of man . . . hath in it a raging and inextinguishable thirst," wrote Henry Scougal in the seventeenth century. "Never doth a soul know what solid joy and substantial pleasure is till, once being weary of itself, it renounces all property [and] gives itself up to the Author of its being."[2] *A raging, inextinguishable thirst!*

Blaise Pascal, a philosopher of the same century, added his voice to those who knew that only God can satisfy the human heart. He said that man tries ineffectually to fill the empty void of his soul by his surroundings: "So he vainly searches, but finds nothing to help him, other than to see an infinite abyss that can only be filled by One who is Infinite and Immutable. In other words, it can only be filled by God himself."[3]

Centuries earlier, Augustine had said to God, "The thought of you stirs him so deeply that he cannot be content unless he praises you, because you made us for yourself and our hearts find no peace until they rest in you."[4] He wrote from experience. As a result of the prayers of his mother and the reading of Scripture, Augustine, an immoral, hardened sinner, was soundly converted. And he discovered in God the answer for the restlessness within.

Perhaps the Psalms give us the most eloquent description of this "raging thirst": "As the deer pants for streams of water, so my soul pants for you, O God" (Ps. 42:1); "O God, you are my God, earnestly I seek you; my soul thirsts for you, my body longs for you, in a dry and weary land where there is no water" (Ps. 63:1).

Mankind has always sought God, but in our pluralistic age, we must ask, *which God shall we seek?* Where shall we find Him? And how shall we know that we have found Him?

## FROM GOD TO IDOLS

"I believe in God" is perhaps one of the most meaningless statements we can make today. The word *God* has become a canvas on which each is free to paint his own portrait of the divine; like the boy scribbling at his desk, we can draw God according to whatever specifications we please. For some He is "psychic energy"; for others He is "whatever is stronger than I am" or "an inner power to lead us to deeper consciousness." To say "I believe in God" might simply mean that we are seeing ourselves in a full-length mirror.

So how shall we begin our journey to find God?

The Swiss theologian Karl Barth was right when he said there are only two ways to attain a knowledge of God: one is to begin with man and reason upward; the other is to begin with God and accept His revelation to us.

For the moment, we are going to begin with man and reason upward. We will uncover some concepts of God that are unworthy of Him: ideas constructed from within the heart of man, idolatrous images manufactured from the raw desires of the human mind. Writes Donald McCullough: "When the true story gets told, whether in the partial light of historical perspective or in the perfect light of eternity, it may well be revealed that the worst sin of the church at the end of the twentieth century has been the trivialization of God. . . . We prefer the illusion of a safer deity, and so we have pared God down to more manageable proportions."[5]

The "trivialization of God"! A "safer deity"! A "God of more manageable proportions"! What shocking accusations. But read on.

Whenever we begin with man and reason upward, we manufacture an idol. Our temptation is to invite ideas of God into our minds that are either just wrong or are notions that diminish Him. Idolatry is more than dancing around a statue of silver or gold; it is constructing a mental idea of a deity that bears little resemblance to the God who actually exists. Idolatry is giving respectability to our own opinions of God, formed after our likeness. Idolatry is fashioning an idea of God according to our inclinations and preferences. It is to pare God down to "more manageable proportions."

In the Old Testament, the psalm-writer contrasted idols with the

God he had come to know through personal revelation. Notice the difference:

> Our God is in heaven;
>> he does whatever pleases him.
> But their idols are silver and gold,
>> made by the hands of men.
> They have mouths, but cannot speak,
>> eyes, but they cannot see;
> they have ears, but cannot hear,
>> noses, but they cannot smell;
> they have hands, but cannot feel,
>> feet, but they cannot walk;
>> nor can they utter a sound with their throats.
> Those who make them will be like them,
>> and so will all who trust in them.
>
> (Ps. 115:3–8)

There are reasons why we prefer our own ideas about God. The Israelites made the golden calf because they became impatient when Moses lingered on the mountain. The delay made them nervous and they wondered whether he would ever return: "As for this fellow Moses who brought us up out of Egypt, we don't know what has happened to him" (Exod. 32:1). God seemed distant and uninvolved; therefore they sought a more present, more realistic god. They fashioned a calf they could see, touch, and carry—a god of "manageable proportions."

This is the first reason why we have so many idolatrous ideas of God today: we are impatient with His silence in this confused age. Donald McCullough quotes newspaper columnist Russell Baxter, who lost his father to an early death, as saying, "After this I never cried again with any real conviction, nor expected much of anyone's God except indifference."[6] We think that if God is all-powerful, He would put an end to the suffering of this world, so we construct a god who puts up with evil for the same reasons we do: he can do very little about it. Or else we turn away from reality and say that evil does not exist.

Let's honestly admit that a growing number of Americans think that the church is irrelevant. Well, that means that the Christian God is seen as irrelevant. What is more, the God of the Bible is exclusive; He appears so demanding that the moment you become acquainted with Him, He begins to raise "sin issues." And because we resent such intrusion, we prefer a God we can manage, not an omnipotent God, but an accepting deity committed to helping us fulfill our human potential.

So a second motivation for idolatry is that we want a God who is more tolerant of us, less demanding, less "judgmental." When a friend of mine left his wife to live with another woman, he withdrew from his friends at the church and formed new friendships in bars and sports complexes. He felt better associating with people who could accept his choices without judging; he wanted to be affirmed, rather than rebuked, for the "courage" to leave his wife. Just so, we want a God who will not mess with the core of our lives.

A commitment to individualism fuels our idolatrous nature. Americans, nurtured on consumerism, go "god shopping" at a spiritual smorgasbord, trying to find a deity that is best suited to their tastes. This cafeteria image is very important: when I select the entrées to suit my tastes, I remain in charge. I might choose something that my mother would want me to have, but then again I might not. Most important, this is my *personal* combination of delicacies, and no choice is better than another. I do not judge the person ahead of me who has chosen an entirely different menu. So I make my selections, forming a conception of God that is "just right for me." And given the wide number of choices on the smorgasbord, any belief system is possible. Millions of Americans say with Thomas Paine, "My mind is my church."

Of course this form of mental idolatry is not a new phenomenon.

5

Centuries ago Asaph recorded these words from God: "These things you have done and kept silent; you thought that I was altogether like you. But I will rebuke you and accuse you to your face" (Ps. 50:21). Yes, even today, we think that God is *like unto us*.

So, the essence of idolatry is to entertain wrong thoughts about God. When we construct an idea of God from our imaginations, this idolatry of the heart is just as bad as idolatry of the hand. The prophet Ezekiel had a penetrating message for this kind of idolaters: "Then the word of the LORD came to me: 'Son of man, these men have *set up idols in their hearts* and put wicked stumbling blocks before their faces'" (Ezek. 14:2–3, emphasis mine). "Idols in their hearts"! "Stumbling blocks before their faces"! No wonder Calvin said that the human mind is an idol factory!

Join me as I explore how our ideas of God affect the way we think, the way we worship, and the way we live. I'm convinced that if our minds are open, our investigation will change the way we see God; and of necessity, it will change the way we see ourselves. And we will be led to seek the true God with all of our hearts.

Let's take a quick tour of some of the idols of modern culture. Let's try to grasp how tempting it is to construct an idea of God based on our own desires and interests.

## IDOLS FOR DESTRUCTION

Of course, some modern conceptions of God are not entirely wrong, just skewed; others are as far from reality as one can travel. Once we assume that we can construct an idea of God beginning with man, that is, "from the bottom up," anything is possible. We are capable of doing this even with our Bible in one hand and a personal agenda in the other.

In *The Trivialization of God,* Donald W. McCullough gives several examples of how we humans redefine our concept of God according to our preferences. I shall choose three of his descriptions and then add some of my own. Though some of these images may be loosely associated with Scripture, others are almost entirely drawn from the fabric of human desires and inclinations.

## The God of My Health and Wealth

Given our preoccupation with success, money, and leisure, we should not be surprised that a special Western god has emerged in the last decades. This concept of God is purported to have been drawn from the Bible, but it reflects American capitalism more than a serious consideration of biblical texts. This God becomes our financial adviser, our ATM, our consultant. Gloria Copeland, wife of minister Kenneth Copeland, has written, "The Word of God simply reveals that lack and poverty are not in line with God's will for the obedient. . . . Allow the Holy Spirit to minister the truth to your spirit until you know beyond a doubt that God's will is Prosperity."[7] She is talking about diamonds, BMWs, and a new house—not spiritual riches.

This gospel could not have been preached in early Rome, nor today can it be preached in Haiti, Belarus, or Angola. It would be difficult indeed to convince the martyrs of the church that it was actually their God-given right to be healthy and prosperous; they would have been content with poverty, if only they had been delivered from the lion's mouth or the assassin's sword.

No, the "God of my health and wealth" is the God of the West, the God of capitalism, the God of consumerism. Correctly interpreted, the Bible can be proclaimed in all cultures; what we say about God must ring true in war as well as peace, in poverty as well as health, in life as well as in death. The "God of my health and wealth" might purport to be based on the Bible, but it is a skewed interpretation that has left thousands of disillusioned people in its wake.

How can we believe in such a God when Jesus said, "Foxes have holes and birds of the air have nests, but the Son of Man has no place to lay his head" (Matt. 8:20)? And Paul, writing from prison, said, "I have learned to be content whatever the circumstances" (Phil. 4:11).

## The God of My Emotional Need

In our therapeutic culture, where all of us are allegedly either in recovery or denial, we have exchanged the language of Scripture for the language of *Psychology Today*.[8] *Sin* is redefined as a lack of self-esteem. Gone is the idea that the knowledge of God is our greatest goal; a knowledge of ourselves and of our need for self-respect should be the first item on our theological agenda. Back in the eighties Reverend Robert Schuller wrote, "What we need is a theology of salvation that begins and ends with a recognition of every person's hunger for glory." According to this conceptualization, God is not a judge who has been offended, but a servant waiting for opportunities to affirm our dignity. Schuller adds, "The Gospel message is not only faulty, but potentially dangerous if it has to put a person down before it attempts to lift him up."[9] Sad to say, these ideas are now a part of our culture and are surviving nicely within the church.

The wider culture suggests that if I can be on a talk show and expose my innermost secrets to the world, I will be helped and healed. I will have my fifteen minutes of fame and "set the record straight." God, if He is worthy of my attention, exists to give me the unconditional acceptance I deserve. In fact, His job is to affirm who I am. My great need is not to repent, but to be comfortable with my true and unique personality. A noted historian Joseph Haroutunian remarks, "Before, religion was God-centered. Before, whatever was not conducive to the glory of God was infinitely evil; now that which is not conducive to the happiness of man is evil, unjust and impossible to attribute to the deity. . . . Before, man lived to glorify God; now God lives to serve man."[10]

In America, sociologist Robert Wuthnow points out, spirituality "no longer is good because it meets absolute standards of truth or goodness, but because it helps me get along in the world. I am the judge of its worth."[11] In other words, God *serves me* as my great cosmic therapist.

There is some truth to all of this. Christ does promise peace, but it is not peace apart from suffering; it is not a peace that is exempt from conflict. Even today, many of Christ's followers are being persecuted and even martyred. His promise is that He will be with us, not that our lives will be free from distress. He came to carry our griefs and sorrows; but when my emotional need for acceptance is more important than my spiritual need for justification, when God owes me fulfillment, when I seek personal gratification more than the humble worship of my Creator—I have forgotten that I exist for His glory and not my own.

How can we reduce God to a recipe for emotional tranquility in light of Jesus' words:

> Do not suppose that I have come to bring peace to the earth. I did not come to bring peace, but a sword. For I have come to turn
>
> "a man against his father,
> a daughter against her mother,
> a daughter-in-law against her mother-in-law—
> a man's enemies will be the members of his own household."
>
> (Matt. 10:34–36)

## The God of My Gender

Radical feminists seek to refashion God according to their desires and inclinations. Here is the argument: God is represented in the Bible as male; males oppress females; thus the biblical model is to blame for this oppression. As long as God is male and seen as our "Father," we give tacit approval to male dominance. To put it simply: if God is male, males are God.

In order to eradicate this image, we must redefine God as female so that we have a deity in step with the feminist cause. Thus Rosemary Radford Ruether, perhaps the leading feminist writer, defines her goddess as "the Primal Matrix, the great womb within which all things, gods and humans, sky, earth, human and nonhuman beings are generated."[12] Some religious denominations now use lectionaries, hymnals, and

Bibles that have "inclusive" language that eliminates all male references to God. Where the title "King" is applied to God, they add the word *Queen;* God as Father is translated "father and mother," or just "mother." Thus the Scriptures are rewritten to serve the feminist agenda.

Let's agree that many men have abused women; males have misused their authority and have put their own needs first. Women have often been unfairly discriminated against in our churches and in the workplace. But do we give God a makeover to address these concerns?

Obviously the God of the Bible has no sexuality; sexuality is confined to the creature, not the Creator. But like it or not, God has chosen to reveal Himself with masculine language. There are reasons for this: for one thing, the Scriptures preserve a clear distinction between creature and Creator. All attempts to remake God as female have resulted in pantheistic ideas about God being one with the creation "she nurtures." Think back to the "Re-imaging" conference held in Minneapolis several years ago. Conference attendees honored the goddess Sophia, not Jesus Christ, as an example of how we can redefine God "from the bottom up." In a follow-up conference, attendees learned that the goddess would emerge when women reveal their inner selves. "Now Sophia, dream the vision, share the wisdom dwelling deep within," they prayed.[13] This is a god created *by* women, *for* women.

Second, in marriage God designated male headship to demonstrate the relationship of Christ and the church. Husbands are to be Christ to their wives, exercising servant-leadership; wives, in turn, are to play the role of the church, living under the authority of their husbands. Given this model, God is represented in the Scripture as male.

In short, society must find ways to address the abuse of women other than rewriting the Scriptures. How can we believe in the "God of my gender" when Jesus affirmed that God created male and female (Matt. 19:4) and that God was Father? "Moreover, the Father judges no one, but has entrusted all judgment to the Son, that all may honor the Son just as they honor the Father. He who does not honor the Son does not honor the Father, who sent him" (John 5:22–23).

A related version is the "God of my sexual preference" theology. This is the view that God approves of my sexual lifestyle, no matter what it might be. There is growing literature on "gay theology," where gay persons have reinterpreted the Scriptures to justify homosexual relationships; they worship God, confident that their sexual preference is of no consequence to Him. For example, Paul Sherry of the United Methodist Church urged his constituents to give full participation to gays and lesbians in the ministry of the church and said that those who opposed this should "read the Bible again with new eyes and listen to the Holy Spirit with new ears."[14] The reason for this new reading is obvious: it is to interpret the Bible in ways compatible with the homosexual lifestyle.

Again we confess that homosexuals have been deeply wounded by the belligerence of the church; they have been singled out for condemnation, almost as if other sins do not matter. Out of their hurt, some reinterpret the Scriptures to make God approve of their sexual preference. But is this the best way to address their concerns? Might it not be more helpful to study not only the biblical condemnation of homosexuality, but also its remarkable teaching about God's grace, mercy, and power?

How can we accept the "God of my sexual preference" when Jesus upheld the strict Old Testament Law? "Anyone who breaks one of the least of these commandments and teaches others to do the same will be called least in the kingdom of heaven, but whoever practices and teaches these commands will be called great in the kingdom of heaven" (Matt. 5:19).

### The God of My Personal Self-Authentication

Lying at the heart of these and other misconceptions is the deeper belief in the "God of my personal self-authentication" theology. An example comes from the book *Conversations with God* in which Neale Donald Walsch supposedly has his questions answered by God Himself. In fact, Walsch claims that in creating this book he was not so much writing as taking dictation.

What does God "say"? We are to reject all authoritative sources, for truth comes to us through our feelings. Walsch's God derides the idea that he/she/it is some omnipotent being that answers some prayers and not others. To quote "God" directly, "Your will for you is God's will for you. You are living your life the way you are living your life, and I have no preference in the matter. This is the grand illusion in which you are engaged; that God cares one way or the other what you do. I do not care what you do, and that is hard for you to hear."[15]

According to Walsch, God says we are not to look to authoritative sources for "the truth about God." Instead, God says, "Listen to your feelings. Listen to your highest thoughts. Listen to your experience. Whenever any one of these differs from what you've been told by your teachers, or read in your book, forget the words. Words are the least purveyor of Truth." Walsch, however, is not clear about how we can distinguish our highest thoughts from our lower ones. And since his God repeatedly says that there is "no such thing as right or wrong, good or bad, better or worse," the matter is even more complicated. Perhaps we find the answer when God says, "There is only what serves you, and what does not." Thus, our highest thoughts turn out to be those that serve *us* the best. Make no mistake; we are our own best authority.[16]

Leaving aside the contradiction that God does not speak in words but feelings (apparently God gives the author a wordy revelation that covers hundreds of pages!), we must ask: why is this God so approving of all of our lifestyles, beliefs, and values? To no one's surprise, this God is exactly everything we want him/her/it to be. This God defines no sin, offers no reproof, tenders no judgment. In fact, there is no right or wrong! After all, in a world without a transcendent God, the word *evil* is emptied of all meaning. Walsch's God has been thoroughly domesticated; as someone has said, we keep cows for milk, sheep for wool, and God to give us continual affirmation and acceptance.

How can we accept the "God of my personal self-authentication" in light of Isaiah's warning: "Woe to those who call evil good and good evil, who put darkness for light and light for darkness, who put bitter for sweet and sweet for bitter. Woe to those who are wise in their own eyes and clever in their own sight" (Isa. 5:20–21). We might add, woe to those who see themselves in a mirror and proclaim that they have seen God!

## The God of My Near-Death Experience

Betty Eadie represents that group of individuals who claim to have learned what God is like through a near-death experience. In her book *Embraced by the Light,* she tells about meeting Christ in the twilight zone between life and death; she even dedicates her book to Him. Now, she says, she knows there will be no judgment at death, just glad admission to the realm that can be best described as a place where everyone is nice. She appeals to the desires of all of us to enter Beulah Land, no questions asked.[17] We also learn that the world is not filled with tragedy as most of us suppose, for humans are not sinful creatures after all.

But how can we believe in the nonjudgmental God of near-death experiences when Jesus predicted that all the dead would be raised and "those who have done good will rise to live, and those who have done evil will rise to be condemned" (John 5:29)?

Ideas similar to Eadie's are found in other popular books, such as *The Celestine Prophecy* and *A Return to Love.* They have common themes: when I encounter God, I am encountering an undefined being who is loving and affirming of who I am. I am a cocreator with God, I participate in the divine; evil is illusionary, and we are all on our way in evolutionary transformation. Such pantheistic ideas, the argument goes, connect us with the ancient masters, and at the end of the day, God is whatever helps me achieve my potential. Such books reduce religion to therapy, and the study of God to little more than a study of myself.

Alan Jacobs, professor of English at Wheaton College, points out that we gravitate to such beliefs because by nature we seek "God's resounding endorsement of our every craving."[18] Thus, as we shout across the chasm to God, His revelation turns out to be the echo of our own voice.

Listen to Jeremiah's cryptic description of such idolatry: "Like a scarecrow in a melon patch, their idols cannot speak; they must be carried because they cannot walk. Do not fear them; they can do no harm nor can they do any good" (Jer. 10:5). In this passage, a couple of characteristics of idols are evident. First, they must be carried—an idol allows me to remain at the center of my life, and my loyalties are always under my control. Second, I can make my idol any shape I desire, and yours can differ from mine; it becomes whatever I make it to be. I can credit it with mystery, with magic, and with meanings derived from my own mind. In the end, since I manufacture reality, I am my own god.

When we construct an idea of God "from man upward" we must, of course, disregard any claims for truth. After all, the God you construct might be entirely different from mine. Hitler had his God and you have yours. Adherents of these new kinds of "faith" can go on triumphantly, fabricating as many conceptions of God as there are cravings in the world. Twenty years ago we heard, "If it feels good, do it." Today, it is "If it feels good, *believe* it."

C. S. Lewis said it more accurately than anyone: "The Pantheist's God does nothing, demands nothing. He is there if you wish for Him, like a book on a shelf. He will not pursue you."[19] The Bible teaches that God created man in His own image; man now attempts to return the favor. No wonder we read of idolaters, "There is no fear of God before their eyes" (Rom. 3:18).

## THE GOD WHO HIDES AND SEEKS

When God spoke to Moses He said, "I AM WHO I AM" (Exod. 3:14). We could paraphrase, "I am who I am and not who you want Me to be." If we stop trying to construct an image of God "from the bottom up" and accept His self-revelation, we encounter a God who is majestic and mysterious, holy and merciful. We find the One who is able to quench our "raging thirst," and we are not afraid to say we have found the truth.

A serious study of the biblical God is countercultural: He stands in sharp contrast to all options on today's spiritual smorgasbord. To be thoroughly biblical is to be controversial; it is to challenge cultural myths that have developed over generations. It is also to be confronted with a God who will not leave us as He finds us.

Regardless of how much we have studied the Scriptures, our knowledge of God is always partial—not false, but *partial*. The more I study the Bible and read what others have written, I am convinced that there is much more about God that we do not know than what we do know.

Take a moment to meditate on this: If His presence fills the universe, is all of His knowledge also spread throughout the universe? Are all of the thoughts *in* His mind always *on* His mind? Since He is both angered and pleased at what is happening in His universe, how does He "cope" with diverse emotions? And do His feelings also pervade the universe simultaneously? You can add your own questions to the list. Our challenge is, as best we can, to "think His thoughts after Him."

We are created in the image of God, but not in His *exact* image. "Now we see but a poor reflection as in a mirror; then we shall see face to face. Now I know in part; then I shall know fully, even as I am fully known" (1 Cor. 13:12). We have but a glimpse of the "vast unknown." John Wesley was right when he said, "Bring me a worm who can understand a man and I will bring you a man who can understand the triune God."

Zophar, speaking to Job in his distress, asked:

Can you fathom the mysteries of God?
Can you probe the limits of the Almighty?

They are higher than the heavens—what can you do?
> They are deeper than the depths of the grave—what can you
> > know?
Their measure is longer than the earth and wider than the sea.

(Job 11:7–9)

To fathom the mysteries of God is life's most rewarding quest.

## The God Who Hides

Isaiah wrote, "Truly you are a God who hides himself, O God and Savior of Israel" (Isa. 45:15). Luther was right when he said that even when God reveals Himself, He still hides. But thankfully, He is also a God who is nearby.

For this is what the high and lofty One says—
> he who lives forever, whose name is holy:
"I live in a high and holy place,
> but also with him who is contrite and lowly in spirit,
to revive the spirit of the lowly
> and to revive the heart of the contrite."

(Isa. 57:15)

In this passage Isaiah describes God's transcendence (greatness in the heavens) and His immanence (His nearness to us). Another prophet recorded God's asking: "Am I only a God nearby, . . . and not a God far away? Can anyone hide in secret places so that I cannot see him? . . . Do not I fill heaven and earth?" (Jer. 23:23–24). An idol is nearby and fills merely the space it takes up; only God is nearby and yet fills the heavens.

It is difficult for us to grasp the transcendence of God. Think of this: Light travels at 186,000 miles a second. Because the sun is 93 million miles away from the earth, the light of the sun takes eight minutes to arrive on our planet. But, in comparison, light from the star Betelgeuse in the constellation Orion takes 520 years to reach us![20]

Think back to the time when Martin Luther nailed his ninety-five theses to the door of the Castle Church in Wittenberg on October 31, 1517. The light that left Orion on that day has not yet reached us, but it is on its way, hustling at 186,000 miles a second! Keep in mind that the diameter of Orion is twice that of the earth's orbit around the sun; in fact, the diameter is estimated to be *about* 400 million miles (it is in constant flux). Yet, this is only one constellation among millions of others; the universe is thought to be 10 billion light-years in diameter![21] "How many are your works, O LORD! In wisdom you made them all; the earth is full of your creatures" (Ps. 104:24).

God is not only the omnipotent Creator, but His essence is holiness, that is, purity and separateness. He is entirely beyond us. We have flashes of revelation, but in the end we simply can't grasp what Isaiah saw when he had a glimmer of God (Isa. 6:1). Wetness is intrinsic to water, light is intrinsic to the sun, and holiness is intrinsic to God. No matter how we try to imagine God, we always fall short.

The pagan world was always haunted by the unknowability of God. Plato said that if God were to be found, it would be impossible to express Him in terms we could understand. Aristotle spoke of God as the supreme cause that all men dreamed of, but no man could know. The philosophers were right about this: without a revelation, God is indeed unknowable. But thankfully, because of His initiative we can move beyond speculation to personal knowledge. For this God has spoken, and He has not stuttered.

### The God Who Seeks

This hidden God also condescends to where we are. "[I also dwell] with him who is contrite and lowly in spirit, to revive the spirit of the lowly and to revive the heart of the contrite" (Isa. 57:15). In fact, Scripture pictures God as being on a search mission. "For the eyes of the LORD range throughout the earth to strengthen those whose hearts are fully committed to him" (2 Chron. 16:9). He seeks those who desire Him; He dwells with those who are "contrite of heart." "This is the one I esteem: he who is humble and contrite in spirit, and trembles at my word" (Isa. 66:2).

To be contrite means to be broken in spirit by a sense of guilt or a sense of sorrow for one's sins. Our knowledge of God leads necessarily to an overwhelming sense of our own sinfulness. Calvin wrote, "Without the knowledge of God there is no knowledge of self. . . . It is certain that man never achieves a clear knowledge of himself unless he has first looked upon God's face, and then descends from contemplating him to scrutinize himself."[22]

As children we receive our sense of self-worth from parents who either reject or love us. We gauge our value from them and the other people around us. As we develop a sense of God-consciousness, we revise our estimate of who we are in relation to our Creator. Unfortunately, New Age theology gives us no reference point; it offers no basis upon which we can properly understand or judge ourselves. This is why a book such as *One Day My Soul Just Opened Up* by Iyanla Vanzant can portray such an optimistic picture of humanity. Modern spirituality goes to great lengths to show that we are all perfect and beautiful. As long as I use my soul to judge my soul, I think myself to be quite fine.

Recently I sat next to a woman on a plane who took modern spirituality seriously. She insisted that sin and evil did not exist. Even Hitler wasn't all bad; he made some mistakes and "unwise choices" but committed no sins, no crimes, no evil. No wonder she felt no need for a redeeming God; her god was no more righteous than she was. I couldn't help but think, however, that if she herself were on the receiving end of a violent crime, she would revise her belief in the nonexistence of evil; and someday, I believe, she will also revise her opinion of her own goodness. But that day, she was like the factory that set the time of its siren by the town clock; later it was discovered that the town clock was checking its time by the siren of the factory!

What has gone wrong in our world? With the loss of the biblical God has come the loss of sin; with the loss of sin comes the loss of a yardstick for behavior. With this loss comes the breakdown of society. A few years ago there was an editorial in the *New York Times* that reflected on the moral confusion of our world:

> Sin isn't something that many people, including most churches, have spent much time talking about or worrying about through the years of the [cultural and sexual] revolution. But we will say this for sin; it at least offered a frame of reference for personal behavior. When the frame was dismantled, guilt wasn't the only thing that fell away; we also lost the guidewire of personal responsibility. . . . Everyone was left on his or her own. It now appears that many wrecked people could have used a roadmap.[23]

Job, you will recall, struggled with the problem of why God took his children and health from him even though he had committed no discernible wrongdoing. He longed to hear from God directly, and near the end of his monologue he got his wish. The Almighty spoke to him from the whirlwind. In those moments of spectacular revelation, Job forgot his arguments and cried, "My ears had heard of you but now my eyes have seen you. Therefore I despise myself and repent in dust and ashes" (Job 42:5–6).

Job finally knew who he was and who God was. He had an "identity crisis" that brought healing to his aching heart. When we begin to understand who God is, we know that His intrusion into our lives cannot be ignored. His presence reveals our tainted souls for what they are, but in Him we also find forgiveness and mercy. The majesty of God should not discourage us but invite us to draw near in contrition and humility. Only a God who judges us can save us. *Idols do not judge us, but neither can they redeem us.*

If we are put off by God's holiness, we probably will also be put off by His grace. Before Ted Bundy, who killed twenty-three young women, was put to death for his crimes, the report was that he had accepted Christ as his Savior. If he did (who can know for sure?), he will be in heaven. If Bundy had brutally killed one of my daughters, I would want him to burn in hell. But God thinks differently than we do. He says I can even accept a Ted Bundy if he repents and takes advantage of the sacrifice of Christ. This is grace.

## BEGINNING OUR JOURNEY

We must embark on our journey to know the real God with these promises: "Without faith it is impossible to please God, because anyone who comes to him must believe that he exists and that he rewards those who earnestly seek him" (Heb. 11:6); "Come near to God and he will come near to you" (James 4:8).

Humbly we realize that only what God has revealed is important to us; we do not have to know all of His reasons for His opinions. I do not know why God sometimes does not deliver His people when they cry to Him. I am mystified by the doctrine of an eternal hell. I do not know all the reasons why God chose this world, this plan, though other options surely were open to Him. The scriptural portrait of God will not always fit neatly with our own predispositions. Since it is hopeless to "begin with man and reason upward," the wisest course is to begin with God and accept His revelation to us.

In the fourteenth century an unknown Christian wrote a book titled *The Cloud of Unknowing*. This author, unlike others, stresses what we don't know about God rather than what we do. The gist of his reflection is that in this life, there will always be a "cloud of unknowing" between us and God, and that should not dishearten us but rather assure us in our pursuit of Him. Yes, we see through a glass darkly, but thank God we do see. He wrote:

Do not hang back then, but labor in it until you experience the desire.
For when you first begin to undertake it, all that you find is a dark-

ness, a sort of cloud of unknowing; you cannot tell what it is, except that you experience in your will a simple reaching out to God. This darkness and cloud is always between you and your God, no matter what you do, and it prevents you from seeing him clearly by the light of understanding in your reason, and from experiencing him in sweetness of love in your affection. So set yourself to resist this darkness as long as you can, always crying out after him whom you love. For if you are to experience him or to see him at all, insofar as it is possible here, it must always be in this cloud and this darkness. So if you labor at it with all your attention as I bid you, I trust, in his mercy, that you will reach this point.[24]

How do we undertake this journey? By forgetting all else, separating ourselves from other creatures, and giving ourselves wholly to God. The author emphasizes that we come to know God through contemplation, through the manifest desire of the heart to fix its thoughts on God.

We must, he says, have a love for God that drives us to seek Him in "the darkness of incomprehensibility, leaving behind other attractions and desires."[25] God and God alone can fully satisfy the hunger and longing of our spirit. If we seek Him, God will give us an experience of Himself. Behind the cloud of unknowing is the *divine Presence*.

A man told me about his friend, a Bible college professor who was finally experiencing what he had taught for so many years. When he shared his growing intimacy with God with his colleagues, they appeared distracted and bored. What he said was not new to them; they had learned it all in seminary. As this "God-lover" pondered their response, it was as if the Almighty Himself spoke to him, saying, "Only people who see Me at a distance think they know everything about Me." Yes, the closer we get to God, the more we are amazed at our ignorance.

There is a story about a farmer who repeatedly invited a friend into his apple orchard to taste the fruit and make fresh cider. "To tell you the truth," his friend said, "I have tasted some of your apples and they are sour."

"Which apples?" the farmer asked.

"The ones that fell along the road over your fence," the neighbor replied.

"Ah, yes," said the farmer, "they are sour. I planted them to fool the boys who live around here. But if you will come into the middle of my orchard, you will find a different taste."

On the edges of Christianity are some sour apples—conviction of sin, self-denial, and purity—that keep off the hypocrites and mere religionists. But in the middle of the orchard are delicious fruits. The nearer to God we draw, the sweeter the joy. Our raging thirst for God can be satisfied.

In his excellent book *Desiring God,* John Piper writes, "God is most glorified in us, when we are most satisfied with Him."[26] C. S. Lewis described God as "the all-satisfying object." Bernard of Clairvaux drank from a fountain that quenched the thirst of his soul and wrote:

Jesus, Thou joy of loving hearts,
Thou fount of life, Thou light of men
From the best bliss that earth imparts
We turn unfilled to Thee again.

*(Jesus, Thou Joy of Loving Hearts)*

The pursuit of God is always most satisfying.

## A PERSONAL RESPONSE

Let us resolve to meditate on the self-revelation of God given in His Word. We've learned that God is hidden and far off, but also near, willing to meet the deepest needs of the human soul. If He stands apart from us because of His holiness, He also stands apart because of His mercy.

I've often reflected on Psalm 42, and I encourage you to read it as a personal response to God's invitation to "seek the LORD while he may be found" (Isa. 55:6). Here are a few verses from the psalm, though I hope you read the entire passage in your Bible:

> As the deer pants for streams of water,
>> so my soul pants for you, O God.
> My soul thirsts for God, for the living God.
>> When can I go and meet with God? . . .
> Why are you downcast, O my soul?
>> Why so disturbed within me?
> Put your hope in God,
>> for I will yet praise him, my Savior and my God.
>
> (Ps. 42:1–2, 5)

Before us lies a challenge. We want to know God, but how do we approach Him? What do we bring that we might be accepted? Let's continue the journey.

# Many Paths Lead into God's Presence

WHENEVER I'M SITTING NEXT TO SOMEONE on a plane, the conversation almost always turns from the weather to religion to Christ. A few years ago my wife and I were sitting together when I noticed that the woman across the aisle was wearing a cross necklace. Hoping to stimulate a discussion, I said, "Thanks for wearing that cross. We do have a wonderful Savior, don't we?"

She rolled her eyes and responded, "Well, I don't think of the cross like you do. Just look at this." She showed me that beneath the cross was the Jewish Star of David, and beneath that was a trinket that symbolized the Hindu god Om. "I'm in social work," she told me. "I've discovered that people find God in different ways. Christianity is but one path to the divine." She went on to say that she preferred spirituality to religion, the search for experience to specific beliefs. She believed in a pantheistic god, a force that need not be feared.

Conversations such as these reinforce my belief that spirituality is flourishing and with it a growing confidence that there are many ways to reach God. Creeds are out, feelings are in. Writing in *Time*, screenwriter and Hollywood producer Marty Kaplan says, "What attracted me to meditation was its apparent religious neutrality. You don't have to believe anything; all you have to do is do it. I was worried that reaping its benefits would require some faith that I could only fake, but I was happy to learn that 90% of meditation was about showing up."[1] To be truly spiritual, we are told, a creed is not only unnecessary, but unwanted. "Americans," someone has said, "are busy inventing unorthodox ways of getting where they're going."

Christianity is being so redefined that it is increasingly difficult to distinguish it from Buddhism or other Eastern religious ideas. We can now be spiritual without God, without "beliefs." And with this drift to pantheism, we also have growing intolerance toward historic Christianity. At a state university a sign read, "It is OK for you to think you are right. It is not OK for you to think someone else is wrong." In the last decade sin has been defined out of existence, but if one sin still exists, it is thinking someone else is wrong. Truth, we are told, is not something to be discovered; it is something to be made up, something to be manufactured either individually or by consensus. One's feelings are more important than, say, the words of Jesus.

Our pluralistic culture rejects outright the claim that God can be approached in only one way. All that the Southern Baptists have to do is ask their members to pray that their Jewish friends would recognize Christ as their Messiah, and a storm of protest erupts. The unity of all the world religions seems like such a worthy goal that those who oppose it are perceived as arrogant, bigoted, and yes, intolerant.

When I was in college, belief in God among the intellectual elite was thought to be antiquated; students and faculty alike patronizingly referred to it as a relic of simpler, less sophisticated times. But the secularism that reigned at the time left a vacuum in the human soul, and thus our cultural pendulum has swung back toward spirituality, though now it's a New Age one.

If secularism banished God from the heavens, spirituality has found God among us. In fact, according to current spiritual thought, He is in everything around us. The Creator is no longer sacred; the creature is. We are told our self is sacred, the earth is sacred, animals are sacred, and so on. In his book *Your Sacred Self* Dr. Wayne W. Dyer writes that he wants to introduce us to "that glowing celestial light and to let you know the wonder of having your sacred self triumph over the demands of the ego self, which wants more than anything to hold you back."[2] Such thinking attributes the glory that should be reserved for God to His creation, just as Paul described: "Although they claimed to be wise, they became fools and exchanged the glory of the immortal God for images made to look like mortal man and birds and animals and reptiles" (Rom. 1:22–23).

Contemporary spirituality defines God as an equal-opportunity employer, the universal source of energy, waiting to be tapped by all of us. What we believe is not important; the challenge is to understand ourselves in light of this higher power that is already within us. If we need forgiveness, we must simply grant it to ourselves; we have broken the commands of no personal God. Since there is no God to offend, there is no God whose forgiveness we must seek. *The craze is self-salvation by self-knowledge.*

Imagine feeling guilty and yet being committed to a religion that teaches that good and evil do not exist! World War II veteran Glenn Tinder tells how his conscience was deeply troubled when he shot two Japanese soldiers in the war. Though he thought they were armed, he was wrong; the deed haunted him. But he had been brought up in the Christian Science religion, which has many resemblances to New Age thought: evil does not exist, sickness is a illusion, and forgiveness from God is unnecessary. Prior to his war experience, Tinder thought of God as "merely the one who had created a good universe and then conveniently disappeared, leaving the human race to 'know' the truth about it and enjoy it." But as he thought about the men he had killed, the word *murder* entered his mind. He knew he had committed an offense: "Now unexpectedly, an angry God—or at least a divine and implacable law, menacing and offended—towered over me. Christian Science gave me no help all: *denying evil, it had nothing to say about forgiveness.*"[3] For decades Tinder sought the truth and eventually embraced Christ, who forgave his sin and cleared his conscience.

Counselors confirm that simply telling ourselves we are fine and need no forgiveness from God will not mute the stifling feelings of guilt. Medical researchers have long realized that people use much psychic energy to neutralize the troubled conscience and the distracted mind that come from the nagging suspicion that all is not well with us.

The German philosopher Nietzsche faced the implication of disbelieving in a transcendent God; indeed, he asserted that God was dead, killed at the hands of man. Therefore he asked:

> How shall we, the murderers of all murderers, comfort ourselves? What was the holiest and most powerful of all that the world has yet owned has bled to death under our knives. Who will wipe the blood off us? What water is there for us to clean ourselves? What festivals of atonement, what sacred games shall we have to invent? Is not the greatness of this deed too great for us? Must not we ourselves become gods simply to seem worthy of it?[4]

To put this in modern context, we could say, "We have redefined God, we have stolen His transcendence, His personhood, and now there is no one left to tell us that we are forgiven!" And yet it is forgiveness we need. In his book *What's So Amazing about Grace?* Philip Yancey tells the story of a prostitute who was homeless, sick, and poor. Through sobs and tears she confessed that she had been renting out her two-year-old daughter to men who wanted kinky sex! She had to do it, she said, to support her own drug habit. When asked why she did not go to a church for help, she replied, "Why would I ever go there? I already feel terrible about myself. They'd just make me feel worse."[5]

Is it fair to say that the church would make her "feel worse"? Perhaps, for a time, but only that she might feel much better. Jesus would say that there is more hope for this woman than for those who think they have no reason to "feel worse." The gods of pop culture have little to say to this poor woman, except perhaps that she should mend her ways and do better next time. Thankfully, the God of the Scriptures does more than that: He offers forgiveness, a clean conscience, and the indwelling of His Spirit. Here is a woman who needs more than to be told that her self is sacred; she needs more than a God who will "affirm who she is." She needs the transcendent God to say, "You are forgiven."

In the next few paragraphs we shall speak of the severity of God, His uncompromising holiness and even anger. But later we shall speak of the grace of God, His acceptance of vile, undeserving sinners. The word *holiness* awakens our consciousness of sin, but God does not leave us there. He picks us up, makes us clean, and gives us the gift of righteousness that we truly need. In the end we will "feel better"—*much* better!

## APPROACHING GOD

The Bible has two warnings for us. First, it warns against remaking God according to our liking. "You shall have no other gods before me" (Exod. 20:3) is the first commandment. The words were freshly chiseled on Moses' tablet of stone when the Israelites violated the commandment by fashioning a golden god in the form of a calf. As we learned in the previous chapter, today we commit idolatry by setting up an idol in our hearts.

But—and this is important—it is not enough that we eschew idols and come before the true God; we must approach Him in the right way. Even in evangelical churches we often hear that it does not matter how we come to God, just that we come. But some people in the Bible learned otherwise.

Cain and Abel disagreed on how to worship God. Abel brought the sacrifice from the firstlings of his flock; Cain was more creative, thinking he could come to God in whatever way he pleased. But God cared little about how much his offering cost him; he did not bring the correct offering, so he was rejected (Gen. 4:5). The New Testament speaks of those who "have gone the way of Cain," that is, those who think they can make themselves worthy to come to God. But Cain learned that procedures are important.

Nadab and Abihu were Aaron's sons and Moses' nephews. They

were consecrated to God, the seminary students of the day, training for "full-time ministry." One day they offered to the Lord "unauthorized fire," and God replied in kind: "So fire came out from the presence of the LORD and consumed them, and they died before the LORD" (Lev. 10:2).

We are tempted to charge God with overreacting. These were young men who deserved a second chance; furthermore, they were sons of Aaron, the high priest. We would expect a bit of leeway. But right there at the altar of God, Nadab and Abihu faced immediate annihilation— no trial, no second chance.

Why did God do this? God Himself explained: "Among those who approach me I will show myself holy; in the sight of all the people I will be honored" (Lev. 10:3). Moses asked two men to retrieve the men's bodies and carry them to their burial; we read that they were still wearing their tunics. Moses told Aaron that he had better not create a scene over this incident or he might die too. He was not to leave the Tent of Meeting but to stay there until calm returned to the area.

Not everything is sacred, but God is. Your self is important, but it isn't sacred; the earth is important, but it isn't sacred. The mistake of these men was not that they came to the wrong God; they just approached the right God in the wrong way. They thought they could dispense with the instruction book. But they learned the hard way that just any way will not do.

If we approach God incorrectly, not much else matters. We might not be smitten down in this life (I will list the reasons in the next chapter), but in the end we will experience eternal judgment. Think of the surprise of those who expected to be in heaven, but find themselves on the wrong side of the celestial gates!

So how do we approach God? The good news is that the issue is not the greatness of our sin, but rather the value of God's prescribed approach. We are invited to come into the "Most Holy Place," but we cannot come alone. Keep in mind that God did not choose the attributes He has. His holiness, justice, and power are a given; He must be true to Himself. We dare not fall into the error of emphasizing the compassion

of God to the exclusion of His justice and holiness. Nor dare we emphasize His justice and holiness without balancing these attributes with His
love and mercy. The omnipotence of God without mercy is terrifying;
the holiness of God without grace leads to despair.

"Don't worry about me, because I am OK," a man told me on a
plane. I had explained that he needed a mediator between him and the
Almighty, that apart from the proper sacrifice God would reject him.
But he thought he was in fine shape because he worshiped his own mental idol, a god who assured him that all was well. He could appear before
the god of his own making with confidence; having never been confronted with the holiness of God, he, like other postmoderns, had lost
the capacity to despise his sin.

Because God is holy, sin is a personal affront to His beauty, His holiness, and His character. If we think we can approach Him directly, it is
because we do not understand Him or ourselves. Augustine was right
when he said, "He who understands the holiness of God despairs in trying to appease him." Making a similar point, Donald McCullough
writes, "One may appear before other gods with a sense of confidence,
with no sense of being threatened. They will stay put; they don't stray
from the places assigned to them by human egos desperately trying to
maintain control. But the God revealed in Jesus Christ is holy, and a
holy God cannot be contained or tamed. This sort of God is 'wholly
other.'"[6]

## FOLLOWING PROTOCOL

I'm told that when visitors have an audience with a king or queen, they
are briefed on expected procedures. It would be strange indeed if God
could be approached directly, without any thought given to the infinite
chasm that exists between us and His holiness. The more unlike us God
is, the more attention we must pay to how we approach Him.

God has meticulously spelled out the proper way for us to come
into His presence. Let us review a bit of data from the Old Testament. In

those times, the high priest went into the Holy of Holies one day a year—the Day of Atonement. The Holy of Holies, you will recall, was a small room in which God localized His presence. True, God exists everywhere, but this was the place where He chose to reveal His glory on earth. When a priest prepared to enter the holiest room, according to the historian Josephus, a rope was tied around his ankle. That way, if he failed to follow procedure and God struck him down, the other priests could pull him out without having to go into the room themselves. Yes, you follow the prescribed path.

I've had the privilege of leading tours to the sites of the Reformation. At least four times I have stood behind the table in Erfurt where Martin Luther offered his first Mass. I always relate how midway through, he froze. Beads of perspiration formed on his forehead. Paralysis struck him as he began to say the words, "We offer unto thee, the living, the true, eternal God . . ." Later he explained:

> At these words I was utterly stupefied and terror-stricken. I thought to myself, "With what tongue shall I address such majesty, seeing that all men ought to tremble in the presence of even an earthly prince? Who am I, that I should lift up mine eyes or raise my hands to the divine Majesty? The angels surround him. At his nod the earth trembles. And shall I, a miserable pygmy say, 'I want this, I ask for that'? For I am dust and ashes and full of sin and I am speaking to the living, eternal and the true God."[7]

Such words are strange to the modern ear. We hear people prattle on about God as if there is no reason to fear, no reason to feel unworthy. Such audacity only proves that those who are truly blind cannot appreciate the light; those who are dead do not feel the weight of sin that resides in their souls. When Moses longed to see the glory of God, the word was, "No man can see Me and live." Today, modern man self-confidently trapezes into the presence of God without the slightest thought that it might be a bad idea.

Why do we need to follow the rules? First, because the moral distance between us and God is infinite. When it comes to matters of purity, God and man share no common ground. The seraphim cried, "Holy, holy, holy is the LORD Almighty; the whole earth is full of his glory" (Isa. 6:3). Holiness is God's most distinctive attribute. We've already learned that everything about Him is holy: His love is a holy love; His anger is a holy anger; His justice is a holy justice.

Then there is the gap between us and God's majesty and greatness. His purposes are beyond us; His intentions are hidden, except insofar as he reveals them. Our first question is not whether He agrees with us, but whether we come to Him in a way that agrees with Him. It is not we who must be pleased; it is He.

How, then, do we reach Him? The consistent teaching of the Bible is that we cannot reach up to Him if He does not first reach down to us. The Old Testament prescribed a ritual by which man was to approach God. The ritual's purpose was to teach the people about God's holiness and the need to approach Him as specified. In the New Testament that Mediator has come.

## AN ACCEPTABLE MEDIATOR

All entrance into the presence of God is mediated; that is, we need someone who can represent our interests as well as those of the offended party, who in this case is God. Similarly, it is practically impossible for an ordinary citizen to get the ear of the president of the United States on his own. He needs someone who knows the president, someone who has an "inside track," to make the connection. God, of course, is the President of the universe, and we have offended His justice.

In Old Testament times the priests were chosen to serve as mediators, but because they were sinners their work was ineffective for final absolution of sin. They represented Christ, who would eventually "take away the sin of the world," as John the Baptist put it. Read this passage, keeping in mind the contrast between the priests of the Old Testament and Christ.

> Day after day every priest stands and performs his religious duties; again and again he offers the same sacrifices, which can never take away sins. But when this priest [Christ] had offered for all time one sacrifice for sins, he sat down at the right hand of God. Since that time he waits for his enemies to be made his footstool, because by one sacrifice he has made perfect forever those who are being made holy.
>
> (Heb. 10:11–14)

In the Old Testament many priests offered sacrifices; in fact, they worked in shifts. But Christ, who lives forever, offered *one* sacrifice *for all time.* The previous sacrifices could take care of only past sins, which is why they had to be reoffered. But we read of Christ, "By one sacrifice he has made *perfect forever* those who are being made holy" (v. 14, emphasis mine). The priests of the old order were not allowed to sit down while working their shift. But Christ sat down at the right hand of God the Father because His work was finished!

When Job was struggling in the heat of the arguments with his "friends," he blurted out that he would desperately like to speak directly to God, not just pray, but dialogue with God face to face. In despair he cried, "He is not a man like me that I might answer him, that we might confront each other in court. If only there were someone to arbitrate between us, to lay his hand upon us both, someone to remove God's rod from me, so that his terror would frighten me no more" (Job 9:32–34). Oh, for a mediator!

A visitor in church told me, "I try to get through to God but am not sure whether the connection is actually made." Think of how wonderful it would be if we had someone who would "make the connection"—someone who was like us but sinless, someone who would represent us to God and represent God back to us. Candidates for the position must have the attributes of God so that the moral and spiritual gap between God and us could be confidently bridged. Christ alone has these qualifications. "Such a high priest meets our need—one who is holy, blameless, pure, set apart from sinners, exalted above the heavens" (Heb. 7:26).

Christ is like us, fully man; He also is fully God. Indeed, someone has said, "A savior not quite God would be like a bridge broken at the farthest end." Not only does Christ represent us in heaven, but we are already there with Him, legally speaking: "God raised us up with Christ and seated us with Him in the heavenly realms in Christ Jesus" (Eph. 2:6). We can access God only on the coattails of the one Man who has the right to enter into His presence.

Perhaps now we understand why there are not many ways into God's presence. Only one Person is able to meet God's requirements for a mediator. Only one Person can give us the perfection we need to stand with confidence in the presence of the Almighty: "I am the way and the truth and the life. No one comes to the Father except through me" (John 14:6).

I know you've heard someone say, "I have not left Christianity but just moved beyond it into spirituality." This is a popular "progression" these days. But strictly speaking, if you move "beyond" Christianity, you must abandon it. Whenever you try to add to it, you subtract from it. Those who surrender the uniqueness of Christ do not simply abandon a part of the gospel message; they abandon the whole of it. Mathematics, like all truth, reminds us that there is only one way to be right, but many ways to be wrong.

If our faith is in Christ, we can expect no complications at the border when we make the journey from earth to heaven. Our Representative is already there, seated in our stead, assuring that we have a safe arrival. God does business with us by doing business with Christ. To stand in the presence of God without representation would be like standing a hundred yards from the sun; God's holiness would liquefy us. "For there is one God and one mediator between God and men, the man Christ Jesus, who gave himself as a ransom for all men—the testimony given in its proper time" (1 Tim. 2:5–6). Let us not dare to think we can enter God's presence alone.

## AN ACCEPTABLE SACRIFICE

Why is a sacrifice necessary for the atonement of sin? Justice demands it. A simple traffic ticket cannot be forgiven without a payment. We are guilty of serious infractions of God's law; indeed, we are an offense to His holiness. Thus we cannot enter unless God's wrath is turned away. "By one sacrifice he has made perfect forever those who are being made holy" (Heb. 10:14): in the presence of Christ we stand both guilty and accepted; unworthy, yet honored.

There are some sacrifices God will not accept. One is the gift of *sincerity;* some think God should receive them because they mean well. Another is the gift of *service;* some remember all the good they have done and think God owes them acceptance for their basic decency. A third is the gift of their own *spiritual quest.* And many bring the gift of *guilt;* they flagellate themselves, believing that if they feel sorry enough, they will pay for their own sins and God will accept them.

Martin Luther has a word for such people: "What makes you think that God is more pleased with your good deeds than he is with his blessed son?" Yes, we must bring an offering, a sacrifice to God, but it cannot be of our own making if we are to win His approval. *It must be the sacrifice He Himself made for us.*

A sacrifice must be equal to the offense committed. Because our sin is against an infinite God, we need a sacrifice of infinite value. It follows that only God can supply the sacrifice that He Himself demands. That is the meaning of the gospel: God met His own requirements for us. Remember the story of the defendant who stood in the presence of a judge for a speeding violation, and the judge himself came down from his chair and paid the fine? That is the story of what God did for us.

Christ's death on the cross repaired the irreparable. "Christ died for sins once for all, the righteous for the unrighteous, to bring you to God"

(1 Pet. 3:18). There is no unpardonable sin for those who cast themselves upon God's mercy in the work of Christ.

The prostitute I referred to a few pages back, the rapist who wrote me from prison asking whether he, too, could be forgiven—both of these and a host of others can be accepted as fully by God as anyone else. The reason is obvious: since God has promised to receive all who trust in His Son, they all receive the same gift of righteousness; they all become members of the same family.

Augustus Toplady had it right:

> Not the labors of my hands
> Can fulfill thy laws' demands
> Could my zeal no respite know,
> Could my tears forever flow
> All for sin could not atone;
> Thou must save and Thou alone.
>
> *(Rock of Ages)*

Recently several from our church staff were riding in a cab, telling a man who was a Muslim why he should accept Christ not just as a prophet, but as the only qualified Savior. He said, "No, I have to pay for my sin. I'm not supposed to get drunk, but I have; I was not supposed to sleep with women, but I have. So justice requires that I suffer in hell for my sins, and after I have paid for them, I will go to heaven."

We told him how glad we were that he was wrong. For one thing, he cannot pay for his sins, even in hell; those who are unforgiven by God are eternally guilty. For another, the good news is that Jesus already paid the debt for those who choose to believe in Him. With all due respect, Muhammad was not able to make such a payment, nor was Krishna, Gandhi, or Zoroaster. You can't put Christ on the same shelf as these other teachers. Only in Christianity do we find that the mediator and the sacrifice are the same person. With Him at our side, we dare to "draw near to God."

## AN ACCEPTABLE ATTITUDE

Let's read carefully our invitation into God's presence:

> Therefore, brothers, since we have confidence to enter the Most Holy
> Place by the blood of Jesus, by a new and living way opened for us
> through the curtain, that is, his body, and since we have a great priest
> over the house of God, let us draw near to God with a sincere heart in
> full assurance of faith, having our hearts sprinkled to cleanse us from
> a guilty conscience and having our bodies washed with pure water.
>
> (Heb. 10:19–22)

We come with our mediator and our sacrifice; we come with the knowledge that we belong to Him and He belongs to us. We come with a sincere heart, that is, with truthfulness and honesty. We come with openness, though we have much that we would prefer to hide. We come fully known, completely exposed, totally understood. We come without trying to put the best spin on our sins and the lives we lived.

We also come with "full assurance," confident that we will be received. Christ is fully accepted, and therefore, we are too. Here we join hands with other sinners: the religious zealot stands with the prostitute; the righteous churchgoer finds himself alongside the murderer. Rather than driving us away from God, our guilt has driven us toward Him. The more clearly we see our sin, the more clearly we must see the wonder of Christ's sacrifice and intercession.

"Therefore, since we have been justified though faith, we have peace with God through our Lord Jesus Christ, through whom we have gained access by faith into this grace in which we now stand" (Rom. 5:1–2). Paul means much more than the fact that we have God's ear when we come to Him through Christ. The word *access* means that we are brought directly into the citadel of God's presence; we stand in the Holy of Holies.

Many years ago two of my daughters and I were in Washington, D.C., where I spoke at a church retreat. Present for the weekend was a member of President Bush's secret-service detail. He asked us whether we wanted to visit the Oval Office the next day, since the president was out of town. We were honored to accept.

The next morning we met at one of the gates at the White House. When we stopped at the first guard station, one of my daughters offered her purse to the officer for inspection, but he waved her on. "You are with him," he said, nodding to the agent, "go on in."

Then, as we entered the White House, we met another assembly of guards. They looked at the agent, glanced at us, and said, "You are with him. Go on in." In the hallway we met more guards. Again they looked at the agent, glanced at us, and said, "You are with him. . . . Go on in."

By now we were nearing the Oval Office; I could already see the open door. One more guard stood at the entrance. Glancing at the agent, he, too, waved us on toward the door with the understanding, *You are with him. Go on in.* Then we set foot in the Oval Office, though we were not allowed to walk far beyond the doorway.

Now imagine that all believers in Christ were to die together. When we arrive on the other side of the gate called death, Jesus comes to join us on our journey enroute to our heavenly home. We go past one sentry of angels standing guard on the path to the New Jerusalem. They look at Christ, then glance at us and say, "You're with Him. Go on in."

Then we pass another band of angels and yet another. Each time, they look at Christ and then glance at us and say, "You're with Him. Go on in."

Finally, we near the very dwelling place of God. We are almost blinded by what the Scriptures call "unapproachable light." For a moment we have a flashback, remembering our sins and failures. Among us are women who had abortions; the prostitute referred to earlier is there with us. Former adulterers stand with homosexuals, thieves with the covetous; all of these were redeemed and cleansed by Christ's blood.

Among the group also are many who were spared such evils, though they struggled with similar sins in their minds. The flashback is so powerful, so real, each of us protests, "I can't go in! I can't go in!"

But the angels at the gate of the dwelling place of God look at Jesus, then they glance at us and say, *"You're with Him. . . . Go on in!"* And so it is that Christ ushers us into the presence of Almighty God.

Don't ever think that there are many ways to the divine. Jesus is the one qualified mediator, the only qualified sacrifice, and the only qualified Savior.

## A PERSONAL RESPONSE

If our trust is in Christ, we will share His triumph in heaven. The following description is a powerful reminder that there is only one Man at the center of the universe, one Man who is able to bring us into God's presence. John's Book of Revelation records the praise offered this man:

> "You are worthy to take the scroll
> and to open its seals, because you were slain,
> and with your blood you purchased men for God
> from every tribe and language and people and nation.
> You have made them to be a kingdom and priests to serve our God,
> and they will reign on the earth."
>
> Then I looked and heard the voice of many angels, numbering thousands upon thousands, and ten thousand times ten thousand. They encircled the throne and the living creatures and the elders. In a loud voice they sang:
>
> "Worthy is the Lamb, who was slain,
> to receive power and wealth and wisdom and strength
> and honor and glory and praise!"
>
> (Rev. 5:9–12)

Let us thank Him for introducing us to the Father and inviting us to the table for fellowship with Him.

| LIE 3 | God Is More Tolerant Than He Used to Be |

"I'M GLAD NO ONE REALLY BELIEVES the Bible anymore, or they'd stone us." Those were the words of a gay activist, replying to a Christian who was using the Bible to condemn homosexuality. The activist's argument was clear: *Since the penalty for homosexuality in the Old Testament was death, how can you say you believe the Bible? And if you don't believe it, then don't use it to argue against homosexuality!*

How do we answer those who insist that God is more tolerant today than He was in the days of the Old Testament? Back then, the law dictated that homosexuals be stoned to death, along with adulterers, children who cursed their parents, witches, and blasphemers. I have discovered about a dozen different sins or transgressions that Jewish law considered capital crimes in Old Testament times.

Today everything has changed. Homosexuals are invited into our churches; parents are told to love their rebellious children unconditionally; adulterers are given extensive counseling. Yes, murder and incest are still crimes, but witches are allowed to get rich practicing sorcery in every city in America.

We hear no more stories of Nadab and Abihu, struck dead for offering "unauthorized fire." We read no more documented accounts of people like Uzzah who touched the ark contrary to God's instructions and was instantly killed (2 Sam. 6:6–7). Today people can be as irreverent or blasphemous as they wish and live to see old age. As R. C. Sproul has observed, if Old Testament penalties for blasphemy were in effect today, every television executive would have been executed long ago.

Is God more tolerant than He used to be?

We need to answer this question for two reasons. First, we want to know whether we are free to sin with a minimum of consequences. Can we now live as we please, with the assurance that God will treat us with compassion and not judgment? A young Christian woman confided to me that she chose a life of immorality in part because she was sure that "God would forgive her anyway." She had no reason to fear His wrath, for Christ had borne it all for her. Her statement begs the question: can conduct that in the Old Testament received strong rebuke or even the death penalty now be chosen with the sure knowledge that God is forgiving, showering us with "unconditional love"?

At one time Christians in America might have been described as legalists, adhering to the letter of the law. No one would accuse us of that today. We are free—free to ski in Colorado and romp on the beach in Hawaii, but also free to watch risqué movies, gamble, free to be as greedy as the world in which we work—*free to sin*. Is it safer for us to sin in this age than it was in the days of the Old Testament?

There is a second reason we want an answer: we want to know whether it is safer for *others* to do wrong today. If you have been sinned against, you want to know whether you can depend on God to "even the score." The girl who has been raped, the child who has been abused, the person who was chiseled out of his life's savings by an unscrupulous salesman—all of these victims and a hundred like them want to know whether God is so loving that He will overlook these infractions. What is the chance that these perpetrators will face justice? We want God to judge us with tolerance; however, we hope that He will not extend the same patience to those who have wronged us. So we wonder: can we depend on God to be lenient or harsh, merciful or condemning?

Many people decry God's apparent silence today in the face of outrageous and widespread sin. The question is, how shall we interpret this silence? Is God indifferent, or biding His time? Has he changed?

41

In a PBS program hosted by Bill Moyers, *Genesis: A Living Conversation,* the participants agreed that there was development in God. He sent the flood to the world, but then, like a child who builds a sandcastle only to destroy it in anger, God regretted what He had done, felt duly chastised, and so gave the rainbow with a promise to never do that again. Most of the panelists agreed that the Flood was evil; it had no redeemable value. Choose almost any human being at random, and he/she would have been more benevolent than God, they said.

The panel assumed, of course, that the Bible is only a record of what people throughout the centuries have thought about God. So as we evolved to become more tolerant, our conception of God became more tolerant. Thus the New Testament, with its emphasis on love, is a more mature, gracious representation of God. This surely would explain the apparent difference between the Old and New Testaments.

Other religious liberals believe that the Bible reveals two Gods: the wrathful God of the Old Testament and the more loving, inclusive God of the New. Again, this is based on the same premise: as humanity changes, so our ideas about God change. In primitive times men's ideas of God were harsh and unrelenting; in more enlightened times, men's conceptions are more tolerant and loving. This, as we have already learned, is building a concept of God beginning with man and reasoning upward.

There is another possibility. We can affirm that God has not changed, His standards are the same, but He has chosen to interact with people differently, at least for a time. In fact, in this chapter we will discover that the attributes of God revealed in the Old Testament are affirmed in the New. Even in the Old Testament we see the severity of God, but also His goodness; we see His strict judgments, but also His mercy.

The neat division sometimes made between the Old Testament with its wrath and the New Testament with its mercy is not a fair reading of the text. Yes, there were strict penalties in the Old Testament, but there also was grace; in fact, looked at carefully, God appears tolerant. Note David's description of his "Old Testament God":

The LORD is compassionate and gracious,
>    slow to anger, abounding in love.
He will not always accuse,
>    nor will he harbor his anger forever;
he does not treat us as our sins deserve
>    or repay us according to our iniquities.
For as high as the heavens are above the earth,
>    so great is his love for those who fear him;
as far as the east is from the west,
>    so far has he removed our transgressions from us.

>    (Ps. 103:8–12)

The fact is, the same balance of attributes is found in both Testaments. There are compelling reasons to believe that God has not changed a single opinion uttered in the Old Testament; the New Testament might emphasize grace more than law, but in the end God reveals Himself with amazing consistency. Properly understood, the penalties also have not changed. And thankfully, His mercy also remains immutable.

Join me on a journey that will probe the nature and works of God; we will see the magnificent unity between the Old Testament and the New. And when we are finished we will worship as perhaps never before.

## GOD UNCHANGING

Who made God? You've heard the question, probably from the lips of a child, or for that matter, from the lips of a skeptic who wanted to argue that believing the universe is eternal is just as rational as believing that God is eternal. If we don't know where God came from, the argument goes, then we don't have to know where the universe came from.

Of course there is a difference: the universe does not have within itself the cause of its own existence. The living God, and not the universe, has always existed, for He is, as theologians say, "the uncaused cause." We can't get our minds around the concept of an uncaused being, but both the Bible and logic teach that if there were no "uncaused being," nothing would ever have existed, for out of nothing, nothing can arise.

Scripture tells us, "Before the mountains were born or you brought forth the earth and the world, from everlasting to everlasting you are God" (Ps. 90:2). From eternity past to eternity future, God exists, and as we shall see, He does not change.

## God's Nature Does Not Change

God cannot grow older; he does not gain new powers nor lose ones He once had. He does not grow wiser, for He already knows all things. He does not become stronger; He already is omnipotent, powerful to an infinite degree. "He cannot change for the better," wrote A. W. Pink, "for he is already perfect; and being perfect, he cannot change for the worse."[1] "Every good and perfect gift is from above, coming down from the Father of the heavenly lights, who does not change like shifting shadows" (James 1:17).

## God's Truth Does Not Change

Sometimes we say things we do not mean, or we make promises we cannot keep. Unforeseen circumstances make our words worthless. Not so with God: "The grass withers and the flowers fall, but the word of our God stands forever" (Isa. 40:8).

David agreed when he wrote, "Your word, O LORD, is eternal; it stands firm in the heavens. . . . Long ago I learned from your statutes that you established them to last forever" (Ps. 119:89, 152). God never has to revise His opinions or update His plans. He never has had to revamp His schedule.

Yes, there are a few passages of Scripture that speak of God as regretting a decision and changing His mind (Gen. 6:6–7; 1 Sam. 15). In these passages Scripture shows God changing His response to people because of their behavior. But there is no reason to think that this reaction was either unforeseen or not a part of His eternal plan. As J. I. Packer put it, "No change in His eternal purpose is implied when He begins to deal with a man in a new way."[2]

## God's Standards Do Not Change

The Ten Commandments are not just an arbitrary list of rules; they are a reflection of the character of God and the world that He chose to create. We should not bear false witness because God is a God of truth; we should not commit adultery because the Creator established the integrity of the family. "Be holy, because I am holy" is a command in both Testaments (Lev. 11:44; 1 Pet. 1:16). God intended that the commandments hold His standard before us. "Love your enemies, do good to them, and lend to them without expecting to get anything back. Then your reward will be great, and you will be sons of the Most High, because he is kind to the ungrateful and wicked" (Luke 6:35). The command to love the unlovable is rooted in the very character of God.

God's attributes are uniquely balanced. He combines compassion with a commitment to strict justice, describing Himself as "the LORD, the compassionate and gracious God, slow to anger, abounding in love and faithfulness, maintaining love to thousands, and forgiving wickedness, rebellion and sin. Yet he does not leave the guilty unpunished; he punishes the children and their children for the sin of the fathers to the third and fourth generation" (Exod. 34:6–7).

Though we die, nothing in God dies; He unites the past and the future. The God who called Abraham from Ur of the Chaldees called me into the ministry. The Christ who appeared to Paul enroute to Damascus saved me. The Holy Spirit who visited the early church with great blessing and power indwells those of us who have received salvation from Christ. The Bible could not state it more clearly: God has not changed and will not change in the future. The prophet Malachi recorded it in six words: "I the LORD do not change" (Mal. 3:6).

Reverend Henry Lyte had to leave the pastorate in Devonshire,

England, because of poor health. As he bade farewell to his beloved congregation, he shared these words, which many of us have often sung.

> Abide with me: fast falls the eventide;
> The darkness deepens; Lord, with me abide:
> When other helpers fail, and comforts flee,
> O Thou who changest not, abide with me.
>
> *(Abide with Me)*

At the Moody Church where I serve, there is a motto in the front of the sanctuary that reads, "Jesus Christ: the same yesterday, today and forever" (see Heb. 13:8). Yes, the One who changes not abides with us.

## GOD'S ADMINISTRATION HAS CHANGED

How then do we account for the difference between the consequences of disobedience in the Old and the New Testaments? If God cannot be more tolerant than He used to be, why are the Old Testament penalties not carried out? Why does it appear to be so safe to sin today?

God's judgments abide, but His method of managing them has changed. He relates to us differently without altering either His opinions or requiring less of us. He is neither more tolerant nor more accommodating to our weaknesses. Let me explain.

When a four-year-old boy was caught stealing candy from a store, his father gave him a spanking. Let us suppose that the same lad were to steal candy at the age of twelve; the father might choose not to spank him but to give him some other form of punishment, such as a loss of privileges or a discipline regime. If the boy repeated the practice at age twenty, there might not be any immediate consequences pending a future date in court. My point is simply that the parents' view of thievery does not change, but they would choose to deal with this infraction differently from one period of time to another. Rather than lessen the penalty as the child grows older and has more knowledge, his parents might exact a more serious penalty.

Just so, we shall discover that God's opinions have not changed; His penalties are yet severe. But there is a change in the timetable and method of punishment. The more carefully we look at the Scriptures, the more we become aware of the unwavering consistency of God and His intention to punish sin. He hates it just as much today as ever. Thankfully, He offers us a remedy for it.

In Hebrews 12:18–29 we see the unity of God reflected in both Mount Sinai and Mount Calvary. Here, like a diamond, the fuller range of God's attributes are on display. We see that God has not lowered His standards; He will in the end prove that He has not mellowed with age. Those who are unprepared to meet Him face a future of unimaginable horror. No, He has not changed.

This change in management can be represented in three ways. Stay with me—the contrast between Sinai and Calvary will give us the answers we seek.

## The Earthly versus the Heavenly

The author of Hebrews gave a vivid description of the mount at Sinai when he reminded his readers:

> You have not come to a mountain that can be touched and that is burning with fire; to darkness, gloom and storm; to a trumpet blast or to such a voice speaking words that those who heard it begged that no further word be spoken to them, because they could not bear what was commanded: "If even an animal touches the mountain, it must be stoned." The sight was so terrifying that Moses said, "I am trembling with fear."
>
> (Heb. 12:18–21)

On Mount Sinai God's glory humbled Moses and Aaron into silence and worship. God called Moses to the top of the mountain to see the fire, lightning, and smoke. Moses then returned to tell the people that they would be struck down if they came too close to the mountain.

The physical distance between the people and the mountain symbolized the moral distance between God and mankind. Not even Moses was able to see God directly, though he was given special privileges. The word to the people was, "Stay back or be killed!"

Imagine the power needed to shake a mountain! Even today we see the power of God in tornadoes, hurricanes, and earthquakes. God accompanied this special revelation with a physical act that would remind the people of His power and judgment. They were to stand back because He is holy.

There was also a vertical distance between God and man. God came down out of heaven as a reminder that we are from below, creatures of the earth. He is separated; He exceeds the limits. To quote Sproul, "When we meet the Infinite, we become acutely conscious that we are finite. When we meet the Eternal, we know we are temporal. To meet God is a study in contrasts."[3] Imagine a New Ager standing at Mount Sinai, engulfed in bellows of fire and smoke, saying, "I will come to God on my own terms. We can all come in our own way!"

Sinai was God's presence without an atonement, without a mediator. It pictures sinful man standing within range of God's holiness. Here was the unworthy creature in the presence of his most worthy Creator. Here was a revelation of the God who will not tolerate disobedience, the God who was to be feared above all gods.

Now comes an important contrast. The writer of Hebrews affirms, "But you have come to Mount Zion, to the heavenly Jerusalem, the city of the living God" (Heb. 12:22). When David conquered Jerusalem and placed the ark on Mount Zion, this mountain was considered the earthly dwelling place of God and later the word *Zion* was applied to the entire city. Centuries passed and Christ came and died outside of its walls, fulfilling the prophecies that salvation would come from Zion.

Mount Zion represents the opening of heaven, and now we are invited to enjoy six privileges. Look at Hebrews 12:22–24. First, we come to "the heavenly Jerusalem" (v. 22). As believers we are already citizens of heaven. As we have learned, we are invited into the "Most Holy Place" by the blood of Jesus.

Second, the writer says we come to the presence of hundreds of millions of angels "in joyful assembly" (v. 22). We come to celebrating angels whom we join in praising God. Don't forget that angels were present at Sinai too (Gal. 3:19), but the people were not able to join them there; these heavenly beings were blowing the trumpets of judgment. Like God, they were unapproachable.

But now we can join them, not for fellowship, but for rejoicing over God's triumphs in the world. Whereas Sinai was terrifying, Zion is inviting and gracious. Sinai is closed to all, for no one can keep the demands of the law; Zion is open to everyone who is willing to take advantage of the sacrifice of Christ. In Jesus the unapproachable God becomes approachable.

Third, we come to the "church of the firstborn, whose names are written in heaven," that is, the body of Christ (v. 23). Jesus said that the disciples should not rejoice because the angels were subject to them, but rather because their names were "written in heaven" (Luke 10:20). The names of all believers are found there in the Book of Life; all listed there are members of the church triumphant.

Fourth, we come to God, "the judge of all men" (v. 23), for the veil of the temple was torn in two and we can enter "the Most Holy Place by the blood of Jesus" (Heb. 10:19).

Fifth, we come to "the spirits of righteous men made perfect" (v. 23), which probably refers to the Old Testament saints who could only look forward to forgiveness, pardon, and full reconciliation with God. In Christ we receive in a moment what they could only anticipate. In a sense they had to wait for us (Heb. 11:40). The bottom line is that we will be united with Abraham and a host of other Old Testament saints. What a family!

Finally, and supremely, we come to "Jesus the mediator of a new covenant, and to the sprinkled blood that speaks a better word than the blood of Abel" (v. 24). God accepted Abel's sacrifice, but his shed blood could not atone for his sin, much less for the sin of his brother. Jesus' blood, however, is sufficient for us all.

The contrast is clear. Sinai was covered with clouds; Zion is filled with light. Sinai is symbolic of judgment and death; Zion is symbolic of life and forgiveness. The message of Sinai was "Stand back!" The message of Zion is "Come near!"

Look at a calendar and you will agree that Christ splits history in two—we have B.C. and A.D.—but He also splits salvation history in two, even as the veil of the temple was torn from top to bottom. Now that His blood is shed, we can come to God in confidence.

Does this mean that God's hatred for sin has been taken away? Has Christ's coming made the Almighty more tolerant? It's too early in our discussion to draw any conclusions. Let's continue to study the passage, and our questions will be answered.

There is a second way to describe this change of administration.

## The Old Covenant versus the New Covenant

Jesus, we have learned, is the mediator of "a new covenant" (v. 24). What does this mean? If He gave us a new covenant, what was the *old* covenant?

In Old Testament times God made a covenant with the entire nation of Israel. He chose to rule directly through kings and prophets, revealing his will step by step, and expecting them to follow His instructions. The prophets could say, "The word of the Lord came to me" and tell the kings what God's will was. There was no separation between religion and the state, as we know it; the state existed to implement the divine will of God.

Obviously, there was no freedom of religion in the Old Testament era. Death was the punishment for idolatry. "You shall have no other gods before me" was the first of the Ten Commandments given to the nation Israel. If people did not obey, the penalties were immediate and, from our standpoint, severe.

Jesus brought with Him a radical teaching, the idea that it would be possible for His followers to live acceptably under a pagan government. He did not come to overthrow the Roman occupation of Israel; indeed, His kingdom was not of this world. When faced with the question of whether taxes should be paid to the pagan Romans, Christ replied, "Give to Caesar what is Caesar's, and to God what is God's" (Luke 20:25). Yes, believers could pay taxes to a corrupt government, and yes, they could fulfill their obligations to God as well.

There are two major changes inherent in Jesus' teaching. First, God would no longer deal with one nation, but with individuals from all nations. He would now call out from among the nations a transnational group comprised of every tribe, tongue, and people, to form a new gathering called the church. These people would live, for the most part, in political regimes that were hostile to them. But we who are a part of this program are to continue as salt and light, representing Him wherever we find ourselves.

Second, in our era, we are to submit, as far as possible, to worldly authorities; we are to do their bidding unless such obligations conflict with our conscience. Indeed, Paul, writing from a jail cell in Rome, said that we must submit to the governing authorities (in his case, Nero) because they were established by God (see Rom. 13:1).

Our agenda as a church is not to take over nations, politically speaking. Of course Christians should be involved in government as good citizens, but our primary message is the transformation of nations through the transformation of individuals. The early disciples had all of our national woes and more, and yet without a political base, without a voting block in the Roman senate, they changed their world, turning it "upside down," as Luke the historian put it (Acts 17:6, NLT).

When Paul came to the immoral city of Corinth, he taught what surely must have appeared a novel idea, namely, that it was not the responsibility of the church to judge the unbelieving world with regard to their morals, but only to judge them in relation to the gospel, which is "the power of God" (1 Cor. 1:18). To the church he wrote:

I have written you in my letter not to associate with sexually immoral people—not at all meaning the people of this world who are immoral, or the greedy and swindlers, or idolaters. In that case you would have to leave this world. But now I am writing you that you must not associate with anyone who calls himself a brother but is sexually immoral or greedy, an idolater or a slanderer, a drunkard or a swindler. With such a man do not even eat.

What business is it of mine to judge those outside the church? Are you not to judge those inside? God will judge those outside. "Expel the wicked man from among you."

(1 Cor. 5:9–12)

If you work in the unbelieving world and decide not to eat with those who are immoral, greedy, or idolaters, you just might have to eat your lunch alone! Of course we can eat with such people if they do not claim to be believers in Christ. But if a Christian lives this way and we have fellowship with him over a meal, or if we enjoy his company, we are in some sense approving of his sin. To help such see the error of their ways, Paul says don't even eat with them.

Now we are ready to understand why we do not put people to death today as was done in the Old Testament. We have no authority to judge those who are outside the fellowship of believers; the state is to penalize those who commit certain crimes, and those laws must be upheld. But—and this is important—all the behaviors that merited the death penalty in the Old Testament are infractions for which we now discipline believers within the church. We do not have the right to take a life, we do not have the right to inflict physical death, but we can announce spiritual death to those who persist in their sins. Paul instructed the Corinthian church to put the immoral man not to death but out of the congregation (1 Cor. 5:5). Such discipline is our duty.

It is foolish for us to think that we can sin with impunity just because Christ has come. The purpose of redemption was to make possible our holy lives. It is blessedly true, of course, that God does forgive, but our sin, particularly deliberate sin, always invites the discipline of God. We are to pursue holiness, for "without holiness no one will see the Lord" (Heb. 12:14). God has not revised His list of offenses.

A woman said to her pastor, "I am living in sin, but it's different because I am a Christian." The pastor replied, "Yes, it is different. For a Christian, such sin is much more serious." Indeed, God takes our disobedience so seriously that the Scriptures warn: "My son, do not make light of the Lord's discipline, and do not lose heart when he rebukes you, because the Lord disciplines those he loves, and he punishes everyone he accepts as a son" (Heb. 12:5–6).

There is a final and important way to describe the contrast between Sinai and Calvary, and at last we will specifically answer the question of whether God is more tolerant than He used to be.

## Immediate, Physical Judgment versus Future, Eternal Judgment

Continue to read this breathtaking passage.

> See to it that you do not refuse him who speaks. If they did not escape when they refused him who warned them on earth, how much less will we, if we turn away from him who warns us from heaven? At that time his voice shook the earth, but now he has promised, "Once more I will shake not only the earth but also the heavens." The words "once more" indicate the removing of what can be shaken—that is, created things—so that what cannot be shaken may remain.
>
> (Heb. 12:25–27)

We can't miss it: if God judged the people for turning away from Him when He spoke at Sinai, just think of the greater judgment that will come to those who turn away from the voice that comes out of heaven, from Mount Zion! The Jews who heard God speak at Sinai did not get to enter the promised land but died in the wilderness. Their primary punishment was physical death, though for the rebellious there was eternal spiritual death as well. Today God does not usually judge people with immediate physical death, but the judgment of spiritual death remains, with even greater condemnation.

If God judged the Jews, who had a limited understanding of redemption, think of what He will do to those who have heard about the coming of Christ, His death, and His resurrection! If the first did not enter the promised land, those today who reject Christ will forfeit spiritual blessings in this life and will assuredly be severely judged by an eternal death. Imagine their fate!

At Sinai God shook the earth. From Zion He is going to shake the whole universe. "Once more I will shake not only the earth but also the heavens" (v. 26). The phrase is borrowed from Haggai 2:6, where the prophet predicts that God will judge the earth (see Rev. 6:12–14). Everything that can be shaken, which denotes the whole physical order, will be destroyed and only eternal things will remain (see 2 Pet. 3:10).

Don't miss the first principle: *the greater the grace, the greater the judgment for refusing it.* The more God does for us, the greater our responsibility to accept it. The judgment of the Old Testament was largely physical; in the New Testament it is eternal. If you, my friend, have never transferred your trust to Christ for salvation, the terrors of Calvary are much greater than the terrors of Sinai could ever be!

Elsewhere, the author of Hebrews faces directly the question of whether God has relaxed His judgments as we move from the past to the present. If we keep in mind that the law at Sinai is spoken of as accompanied by angels, we will understand his argument, "For if the message spoken by angels was binding, and every violation and disobedience received its just punishment, *how shall we escape if we ignore such a great salvation?*" (2:2–3,). He aruges from the lesser to the greater: if the law demanded exacting penalties, think of the more severe punishment for those who refuse grace!

In a sense we can say that the harsh penalties of the Old Testament demonstrated an overabundance of grace: by seeing these punishments immediately applied, the people had a visual demonstration of why they should fear God. In our day, these penalties are waived, and as a result people are free to misinterpret the patience of God as laxity or indifference.

Today God allows sins to accumulate and delays their judgment. Paul, writing to those who had hardened their hearts against God, said, "Because of your stubbornness and your unrepentant heart, you are storing up wrath against yourself for the day of God's wrath, when his righteous judgment will be revealed" (Rom. 2:5). Retribution and justice have not escaped God's attention. Grace gives the illusion of tolerance and, if not properly interpreted, can be construed as a license to sin. Indeed, the New Testament writer Jude warned that there "are godless men, who change the grace of our God into a license for immorality and deny Jesus Christ our only Sovereign and Lord" (Jude 4). They confuse the patience of God with the leniency of God.

A second principle: *we should never interpret the silence of God as the indifference of God*. God's long-suffering is not a sign of either weakness or indifference; it is intended to bring us to repentance. "The Lord is not slow in keeping his promise, as some understand slowness. He is patient with you, not wanting anyone to perish, but everyone to come to repentance" (2 Pet. 3:9). It would be a mistake to think that His "slowness" means that He is letting us skip our day of judgment. Solomon in Ecclesiastes warned that a delay in applying punishment encourages wrongdoing: "When the sentence for a crime is not quickly carried out, the hearts of the people are filled with schemes to do wrong" (Eccles. 8:11). How easily we misinterpret divine patience as divine tolerance!

In the end, all penalties will be exacted; retribution will be demanded; nothing will be overlooked. At the Great White Throne judgment, the unbelievers of all ages will be called into account and meticulously judged. Those who see a difference between the severity of the Old Testament and the tolerance of the New should study this passage carefully: "The sea gave up the dead that were in it, and death and Hades gave up the dead that were in them, and each person was judged according to what he had done. Then death and Hades were thrown into the lake of fire. The lake of fire is the second death. If anyone's name was not found written in the book of life, he was thrown into the lake of fire" (Rev. 20:13–15). Nothing that terrifying occurs in the Old Testament.

Is it safe to sin? In *The Lion, the Witch, and the Wardrobe,* C. S. Lewis tells the story of four children who encounter a magical world through the back of an old attic wardrobe. In this land, Narnia, animals talk, and one especially glorious creature, a majestic lion, represents Christ. Some beavers describe the lion to Lucy, Susan, and Peter, who are newcomers to Narnia, and they fear meeting Aslan. The children ask questions that reveal their apprehension.

> "Ooh!" said Susan, "I'd thought he was a man. Is he—quite safe? I shall feel rather nervous about meeting a lion."
>
> "That you will, dearie, and no mistake," said Mrs. Beaver, "if there's anyone who can appear before Aslan without their knees knocking, they're either braver than most or else just silly."
>
> "Then he isn't safe?" said Lucy.
>
> "Safe?" said Mr. Beaver. "Don't you hear what Mrs. Beaver tells you? Who said anything about safe? 'Course he isn't safe. But he's good. He's the King, I tell you."[4]

Is God safe? Of course not. "It is a dreadful thing to fall into the hands of the living God" (Heb. 10:31). But thankfully, He is good, and if we respond to Him through Christ, He will save us.

If we still think that God is more tolerant of sin in the New Testament than in the Old, let us look at what His Son endured at Calvary; imagine Him as He languishes under the weight of our sin. There we learn that we must either personally bear the penalty for our sins, or else it must fall on the shoulders of Christ. In either case, the proper and exact penalties shall be demanded. And because we ourselves cannot pay for our sins, we shall have to live with them for all of eternity—unless we come under the shelter of Christ's protection. Only Christ can turn away the wrath of God directed toward us.

Is it true that justice delayed is justice denied? For human courts this is so, for as time passes evidence is often lost and the offender is freed. But this does not apply to the Supreme Court of heaven; with God, no facts are lost, no circumstances are capable of misinterpretation. The whole earthly scenario can be re-created so that scrupulous justice can be satisfied. Judicial integrity will prevail, and we shall sing forever, "Salvation and glory and power belong to our God, for true and just are his judgments" (Rev. 19:1–2).

Is Jesus only, as the old rhyme goes, "meek and mild"? In the same C. S. Lewis story I quoted above, the children meet Aslan the Lion. Lucy observes that his paws are potentially very inviting or very terrible. They could be as soft as velvet with his claws drawn in, or as sharp as knives with his claws extended. Christ is both meek and lowly, but also fierce and just. Read this description of Christ, and you will agree that the warnings of the New Testament are as terrifying as the Old.

> With justice he judges and makes war. His eyes are like blazing fire, and on his head are many crowns. He has a name written on him that no one knows but he himself. He is dressed in a robe dipped in blood, and his name is the Word of God. The armies of heaven were following him, riding on white horses and dressed in fine linen, white and clean. Out of his mouth comes a sharp sword with which to strike down the nations. "He will rule them with an iron scepter." He treads the winepress of the fury of the wrath of God Almighty. On his robe and on his thigh he has this name written: KING OF KINGS AND LORD OF LORDS.
>
> (Rev. 19:11–16)

What follows in this passage is an unbelievable description of the carnage that takes place after Jesus executes His judgment. With sword in hand, He smites His enemies and leaves them dying on the battlefield. Even if we appropriately grant that the account is symbolic, it can mean nothing less than the revelation of the vengeance of God Almighty. The Lord God of Sinai is the Lord God of Zion.

Finally, figuratively speaking, *we must come to Sinai before we come to Zion.* We must see our sin before we can appreciate grace. In the allegory called *Pilgrim's Progress,* a man named Christian travels with the weight of sin on his shoulders, but the burden proves too much for him. Thankfully, he comes to Calvary, and there his load is rolled onto the shoulders of the one Person who is able to carry it. To his delight the terrors of Sinai are borne by the Son at Calvary. What a tragedy to meet people who are comfortable with who they are, people who have not felt the terrors of God's holy law. Since they do not see themselves as lost, they need not be redeemed; absorbed in themselves, they have lost the capacity to grieve over their sin.

To those aware of their need, we say, "Come!" Come to Mount Zion to receive mercy and pardon. Stand at Mount Sinai to see your sin, then come to linger at Calvary to see your pardon. "Therefore, since we are receiving a kingdom that cannot be shaken, let us be thankful, and so worship God acceptably with reverence and awe, for our 'God is a consuming fire'" (Heb. 12:28–29). There was fire at Sinai; there will also be fire at the final judgment. *A consuming fire!*

Donald McCullough writes:

> Fire demands respect for its regal estate. It will not be touched, it will be approached with care, and it wields its scepter for ill or for good. With one spark it can condemn a forest to ashes and a home to a memory as ghostly as the smoke rising from the charred remains of the family album. Or with a single flame it can crown a candle with power to warm a romance and set to dancing a fireplace blaze that defends against the cold. Fire is dangerous to be sure, but we cannot live without it; fire destroys but it also sustains life.[5]

There is a story that comes to us from the early days, when a man and his daughter spotted a prairie fire in the distance. Fearing being engulfed by the flames, the father suggested they build a fire right where they stood. They burned one patch of grass after another, in an ever-widening circle. Then when the distant fire came near, the father comforted his terrified daughter by telling her that flames would not come to the same patch of ground twice; the father and daughter would be safe if they stood where the fire had already been.

When we come to Mount Zion, we come to where the fire of Sinai has already struck. We come to the only place of safety; we come to the place where we are welcome. There we are sheltered from terrifying judgment.

God's Son endured the fire that was headed in our direction. Only those who believe in Him are exempt from the flames.

## A PERSONAL RESPONSE

There is a story about some members of a synagogue who complained to a rabbi that the liturgy did not express what they felt. Would he be willing to make it more relevant? The rabbi told them that the liturgy was not intended to express what they felt; it was their responsibility to learn to feel what the liturgy expressed.

There is a lesson here. In our day some have so emphasized "felt needs" in worship that they have forgotten that in a future day our most important "felt need" will be to stand before God covered by the righteousness of Christ. The real issue is not how we feel, but rather how God feels. Our responsibility is to "learn to feel" what God does.

Let us worship at both of the mountains that are symbolic of the two covenants. We must first come to Mount Sinai as a reminder of our sinfulness; then we stand at Mount Calvary as a reminder of grace.

On the morning of the third day there was thunder and lightning, with a thick cloud over the mountain, and a very loud trumpet blast. Everyone in the camp trembled. Then Moses led the people out of the camp to meet with God, and they stood at the foot of the mountain. Mount Sinai was covered with smoke, because the LORD descended on it in fire. The smoke billowed up from it like smoke from a furnace, the whole mountain trembled violently, and the sound of the trumpet grew louder and louder. Then Moses spoke and the voice of God answered him.

The LORD descended to the top of Mount Sinai and called Moses to the top of the mountain. So Moses went up and the LORD said to him, "Go down and warn the people so they do not force their way through to see the LORD and many of them perish."

(Exod. 19:16–21)

And now we turn to Mount Calvary.

At the sixth hour darkness came over the whole land until the ninth hour. And at the ninth hour Jesus cried out in a loud voice, *"Eloi, Eloi, lama sabachthani?"*—which means, "My God, my God, why have you forsaken me?"

When some of those standing near heard this, they said, "Listen, he's calling Elijah."

One man ran, filled a sponge with wine vinegar, put it on a stick, and offered it to Jesus to drink. "Now leave him alone. Let's see if Elijah comes to take him down," he said.

With a loud cry, Jesus breathed his last.

The curtain of the temple was torn in two from top to bottom. And when the centurion, who stood there in front of Jesus, heard his cry and saw how he died, he said, "Surely this man was the Son of God!"

(Mark 15:33–39)

Let us join with the centurion and say, "Surely He was the Son of God!"

# LIE 4

# God Has Never Personally Suffered

HAS *GOD* EVER SUFFERED?

Jews want to know where God was during the Holocaust; Christians want to know where He was in the massacre of the Armenians; the Kosovars want to know where He was during their bloody civil war. In fact, there is not a person reading this who has not asked that question in the face of tragedy: where is God in the suffering of cancer or the untimely death of a spouse? We also want to know whether He has ever personally suffered—has He entered into the anguish of mankind?

Many people believe that the God of Christianity is indifferent to the sufferings of the inhabitants of this planet. Some believe the gods of New Age religion, the gods of the East, are more compatible with our plight since these deities do not claim omnipotence. A god who resides within us can hardly be responsible for the evils of the world. But the Christian God, the Being who exists independently of the universe, who answers prayer and supposedly created all that is, is more culpable. A God who sees human suffering and fails to intervene is hardly worthy of worship.

What do you say to the owner of such a skeptical view?

Perhaps you would be tempted to remind him of the sun and rain that cause crops to grow so that we might eat. This truth would not convince the skeptic; yes, there are rain showers but also floods, hurricanes, and tornadoes. In some places the earth is firm, but in other countries earthquakes occur frequently. Millions of people enjoy healthy lives, but others die early and painful deaths by starvation, natural disasters, or disease. Take a hard look at nature, and you will never guess that God really cares. It all reminds me of Rodney Dangerfield's quip, "I put a seashell to my ear and got a busy signal."

Or you might be tempted to point the skeptic to mankind. We all know people who care about each other; this must mean that God cares about us. But for every person who is loving, there is someone who is cruel; for every generous person there is one who is greedy. Just look at the headlines of today's paper to see what people do to one another. You'll find scant proof that there is a God who genuinely cares about the world.

Intuitively, we believe that a God who cannot suffer is a God who cannot love. As believers we cannot get a hearing from a cynical world unless we can show that God cares and that because He cares, He not only understands our suffering but also has experienced it Himself.

False religions proliferate, because of cynicism, the conviction that the Christian God has proved indifferent to our plight. Even those who would like to believe conclude that God isn't benevolent, and sadly, it appears that His followers aren't either. Many find Christians to be judgmental, self-serving, and unwilling to be uprooted from their comfortable lifestyles.

C. S. Lewis wrote that he was often on the verge of deception: "Not that I am in much danger of ceasing to believe in God. The real danger is to believe such dreadful things about Him. The conclusion I dread is not 'So there is really no God after all,' but 'So this is what God is really like. Deceive yourself no longer.'"[1]

Do we have some reason not to think some dreadful things about God? Can we say with integrity that God cares and therefore people matter? Only at the cross do we see the love of God without ambiguity. Here is God's farthest reach, His most ambitious rescue effort. God personally came to our side of the chasm, willing to suffer for us and with us. At the cross His love burst upon the world with unmistakable clarity. Here at last we have found solid reasons to believe that there was a genuine connection between God and man. Here is mercy; here is justice. And here is a God who suffers with us.

At the cross, cynicism ends.

Scripture tells us that at Calvary, "God was reconciling the world to himself in Christ" (2 Cor. 5:19). In those nine words we have the essence of the gospel, the assurance that God has drawn near, and the answer to the skeptic's questions. God has built a bridge to us and paid the entire cost of its construction. And He walks arm in arm with us over the chasm, entering into our own suffering. Here we see a God who has Himself faced the cruel blows of what is popularly called fate, though they are blows He predetermined He would bear. Here we meet a God who will astound us and captivate our hearts.

To better understand the suffering of God, we need to take a journey that begins at a familiar stream but ends in the deep river of God's loving-kindness and personalized grace. If we stare at the cross intently, we shall find a God who not only judges but a God who also grieves, a God who not only smites, but also heals—a God who has suffered.

Three common words—*self-substitution, submission,* and *suffering*—will guide us to some uncommon blessings.

## THE SELF-SUBSTITUTION OF GOD

The idea of substitution is as old as Eden, where God killed animals so that Adam and Eve would have a covering for their nakedness. Those animals shed their blood for our first parents in order to picture the coming of a better sacrifice in the distant future. From then on the phrase *in the place of* was the essence of Old Testament theology.

When an angel prevented Abraham from sacrificing Isaac, "in a thicket he saw a ram caught by its horns" (Gen. 22:13). Providentially, Abraham took the ram and offered him up for a burnt offering *in the place of* his son. The very word *sacrifice* implies substitution.

When the Israelites were about to leave Egypt, they sprinkled on their doorposts the blood of a lamb so the angel of death would bypass them. Thus the lamb died *in the place of* the firstborn in every Israelite home.

But these lambs were only symbolic; they were unable to permanently shield the Israelites from judgment or take away the sins of the nation.

The substitute sacrificed has to have a value sufficient to bear the penalty. When God surveyed the universe, He found no sacrifice that would meet the qualifications to redeem humanity. No animal or man qualified. If the barrier of sin that exists between God and us was to be removed, God would have to provide the substitute Himself. Thankfully He did just that.

The prophet Isaiah, writing as though he were sitting at the foot of the cross, described Christ's mission:

> Surely he took up our infirmities
> > and carried our sorrows,
> yet we considered him stricken by God,
> > smitten by him, and afflicted.
> But he was pierced for our transgressions,
> > he was crushed for our iniquities;
> the punishment that brought us peace was upon him,
> > and by his wounds we are healed.
> We all, like sheep, have gone astray,
> > each of us has turned to his own way;
> and the Lord has laid on him
> > the iniquity of us all.
>
> (Isa. 53:4–6)

God, in Christ, chose to bear the penalty that He Himself demanded. God became both our judge and our substitute. He both sentenced us to eternal condemnation and paid that price on our behalf. To quote Charles Cranfield in his commentary on Romans: "God, because in his mercy he willed to forgive sinful men, and, being truly merciful, willed to forgive them righteously, that is, without in any way condoning their sin, purposed to direct against his own very self in the person of his son the full weight of that righteous wrath which they deserved."[2]

Recently I read that a mother threw herself over her two-year-old son to absorb the impact of a car that was out of control. She was killed, but her child lived. She became the substitute, preserving the physical life of the one she dearly loved. She literally died *in the place of* her son. In the same way, God rescued us from the more terrifying fate of eternal moral and spiritual lostness. And He put Himself in harm's way to absorb the blow. Calvin wrote, "This is our acquittal: the guilt that held us liable for punishment has been transferred to the head of the son of God."[3]

On a plane I spoke to a woman who wondered how I could be so sure of my relationship with God. "How can you know that if this plane went down you'd go to heaven?" she probed.

I answered, "I am sure because I am convinced that Christ's sacrifice is all that God will ever require of me to stand before Him. Because the sacrifice was fully accepted, I am fully acquitted." Mrs. H. M. Hall wrote:

> Jesus paid it all,
> All to Him I owe;
> Sin had left a crimson stain,
> He washed it white as snow.
> *(Jesus Paid It All)*

John Stott wrote, "For the essence of sin is man substituting himself for God, while the essence of salvation is God substituting himself for man."[4]

We now move from the familiar to the less familiar. Now we must probe the mystery of the Father-Son relationship and the role of the suffering God.

## THE SUBMISSION OF GOD

In the same chapter quoted earlier, Isaiah portrayed Christ as a willing victim. "He was oppressed and afflicted, yet he did not open his mouth; he was led like a lamb to the slaughter, and as a sheep before her shearers is silent, so he did not open his mouth" (Isa. 53:7). The prophet likened Jesus to a lamb, not because He was weak, but because He was submissive. He could have called angels to deliver Him, but He voluntarily died for us.

Who put Christ on the cross? The Jews did, the Gentiles did, we did; and God did. Here we must avoid an error that we make too easily. Some believe that a benevolent Christ persuaded a reluctant God to do something about the plight of humanity and He grudgingly agreed. The Father then took His anger against sinful humanity and directed it toward Christ.

Those who adhere to this popular understanding of the cross often support it with quotes from this same passage of Scripture, saying that Christ was "stricken by God, smitten by him, and afflicted" (Isa. 53:4) and "yet it was the LORD's will to crush him and cause him to suffer" (Isa. 53:10). The image of an angry God exacting every ounce of payment from a submissive Christ can distort our understanding of the Almighty. If not properly understood in context, we can end up thinking some dreadful things about Him. We will view the Son as loving and willing, but the Father as reluctant and harsh.

Such an interpretation flounders in the face of God's love. Indeed, the saving work of God originated in Him; it is because of the "tender mercy of our God" that Christ came (Luke 1:78). The most famous verse in the Bible teaches that "*God* so loved the world that he gave his one and only Son" (John 3:16, emphasis mine). The Father initiated salvation because of His loving-kindness; the Father is a redeeming God.

The Father and the Son took the initiative together. As John Stott writes, "We must not, then, speak of God punishing Jesus or of Jesus persuading God, for to do so is to set them over against each other as if they acted independently of each other or were even in conflict with each other. . . . The Father did not lay on the Son an ordeal he was reluctant to bear, nor did the Son extract from the Father a salvation he was reluctant to bestow."[5] Stott is right to point out that the will of the Father and the will of the Son coincided in the perfect self-sacrifice of love. We must never view the Son and the Father as being in opposition to each other.

It is true that Jesus cried out on the cross, "My God, my God, why have you forsaken me?" (Mark 15:34). But if the Father turned away from the Son at the cross, it is because they agreed that it must be so, given the plan of redemption that they had chosen.

If Father and Son were unified in their decision to create the world, they were similarly unified in the greater act of redemption. Although the Incarnation invites us to distinguish the persons of the Godhead, it does not allow us to see them in conflict. As we read earlier, "*God* was reconciling the world to himself *in Christ*" (2 Cor. 5:19, emphasis mine). This does not mean that God is our servant; it means simply that given the ends He wanted to accomplish, He chose to accommodate Himself to our great need of redemption. He submitted Himself to our need.

Now we move further downstream, wading in the deep waters of contemplation, trying to understand our suffering God. We must tread carefully, keeping in mind that we are entering into the mystery of the Incarnation and Crucifixion. Our challenge will be to stay within the confines of God's revelation, and yet without fear say, *God* suffered on our behalf.

## THE SUFFERING OF GOD

We now come to the event that is best described as the hinge of history, the one happening that stretches the limits of our understanding. We will contemplate the cross. But before we do so, we must wrestle with the question of whether God can actually suffer.

*Can* God suffer? *Did* God suffer? *Does* God suffer?

In the early centuries of the church, believers spent much discussion on the impassibility of God, that is, the doctrine that He is incapable of feeling pain. He has, some said, no emotions that are affected by what happens on earth; not that He is removed from us or indifferent, but He is simply unaffected by our trauma. It was widely taught that God stays above the fray, granting us His grace but not suffering with us in our pain.

The Westminster Confession of Faith asserts that God is "without body, parts, or passions, immutable."[6] Even some contemporary theologians argue that only the human nature of Christ suffered on the cross, not the divine. The love of Christ, they contend, was the love of God, the power of Christ was the power of God, but the suffering of Christ did not belong to the Godhead. God could not suffer in the Incarnation as the God-man. It was His humanity alone that heaved with emotion the night before His crucifixion.

There were two reasons for this view. First, because God is immutable: "I the LORD do not change" (Mal. 3:6). Emotional ups and downs would be inconsistent with His perfection.

Second, God is self-existent and has within Himself all of the resources He needs for his own pleasure and enjoyment; He does not have to look outside of Himself for pleasures or pain. He cannot be a victim of evil; He cannot be subject to the same fluctuations as we. Therefore the divine nature did not suffer even when Christ died.

Is this biblical?

I certainly agree that it would be dishonoring to say that God is like a child who loses his temper, like a frustrated lover who grieves over the companion who jilted him, or worse, like a lover who wishes his dearest to love him but is incapable of bringing this about. Even more disrespectful would be the notion that God is a victim of His emotions and like us, can't do much about His changeable moods or feelings. A God who suffers because He cannot help it, or a God who suffers because of circumstances beyond His control, would be a pathetic creature unworthy of our adoration.

That said, bear in mind that *God chose to suffer*. He has chosen to be rejected by some and accepted by others; He chose to have His beloved Son suffer in our behalf. As far as we know, God could have willed otherwise; He most likely had before Him an indefinite number of possible worlds in which there were no Fall, no sin, no need for redemption. Yet

He chose this plan with its injustice and pain. We are invited to believe that looked at from eternity, this plan is best (see chapter 8).

As humans, we suffer involuntarily. The circumstances of life, with their mixture of joys and sorrows, are largely out of our hands. But everything is in God's hands, *everything*. He suffers because He willed it to be so; no man can make God suffer. Someone has said, "He suffers by divine consent." We must forever do away with any notion of a weak God who is a victim of the chaos that has resulted from His original creation.

Furthermore, it *pleased* God to suffer. He was not forced into a situation in which He could not find pleasure, for God does whatever He pleases (Pss. 115:3; 135:6).

> But the LORD was *pleased*
> To crush Him, putting Him to grief;
> If He would render Himself as a guilt offering,
> He will see His offspring,
> He will prolong His days,
> And the good *pleasure* of the LORD will prosper in His hand.
> (Isa. 53:10, NASB, emphasis mine)

Paul says the death of Christ was a "fragrant aroma" to God (Eph. 5:2, NASB). If we find it contradictory to say that the Father felt the grief of His suffering at the cross, yet at the same time God was pleased with it, we have not thought deeply enough about the complex nature of God's emotions. Just as we can have joy in sorrow, great comfort in suffering, so the Father was grieved in one sense but pleased in another. Viewed through a narrow lens, He is angry and grieved; looked at from the standpoint of eternity, God is wholly pleased. All of this is because He chose that it would be so. (I will discuss this in more detail in chapter 9.)

The Bible describes God as having deep emotions. He commanded Hosea, you will recall, to marry a woman who would become a prostitute. Hosea's personal feeling of betrayal and loss represented the betrayal and loss God experienced over wayward Israel. You might think that one of the advantages of being God is to never feel disappointment; after all, He has infinite power and nothing can stand in His way. But He can feel grief too. There is no heartbreak like that of unrequited love, and the Almighty planned that He would experience it. Just read these lines and sense the pathos of God.

> "Is Ephraim My dear son?
> Is he a delightful child?
> Indeed, as often as I have spoken against him,
> I certainly still remember him;
> Therefore My heart yearns for him;
> I will surely have mercy on him," declares the LORD.
>
> (Jer. 31:20, NASB)

In another passage God asks, "Can a woman forget her nursing child, and have no compassion on the son of her womb? Even these may forget, but I will not forget you" (Isa. 49:15, NASB). The prophet depicts God's passionate love and burning wrath. God wants to whip the rebellious child and hug him simultaneously. Since we are made in the image of God, it must be that God has emotions. Certainly if the Holy Spirit is grieved because of our sin, we can say the same of the Father.

Centuries ago, Luther complained that the scholar Erasmus had failed to do justice to the majesty of God: "Your God is too human," he said. I'm sure the criticism was valid, for as we have already learned we create an idol when we make God "too human." But it is also possible to have a conception of God that is not human enough. We've all met people whose emotions have been numbed because of abuse or personal tragedy. In my opinion, it would be dreadful indeed if God, like the ancient Greek gods, were incapable of feeling pain or grief.

We come now to one event that most clearly reveals the suffering of God.

## THE SUFFERING OF THE CROSS

From the sixth hour until the ninth hour darkness came over all the land. About the ninth hour Jesus cried out in a loud voice, *"Eloi, Eloi, lama sabachthani?"*—which means, "My God, my God, why have you forsaken me?"

When some of those standing there heard this, they said, "He's calling Elijah."

Immediately one of them ran and got a sponge. He filled it with wine vinegar, put it on a stick, and offered it to Jesus to drink. The rest said, "Now leave him alone. Let's see if Elijah comes to save him."

And when Jesus had cried out again in a loud voice, he gave up his spirit.

(Matt. 27:45–50)

All of course acknowledge that Christ suffered on the cross. His grief in Gethsemane, His expressions of sorrow, and His cries in those final moments testify of His personal agony and pain. What was happening when He died? He became legally guilty of our sin; the spotless One came in contact with genocide, rape, adultery, greed, cruelty, and murder. "He himself bore our sins in his body on the tree" (1 Pet. 2:24).

The Father who loved the Son temporarily abandoned Him, increasing the anguish of the Son. The Father neither intervened nor chose to comfort His Son. The thief crucified next to Christ taunted Him, "Aren't you the Christ? Save yourself and us!" (Luke 23:39). Though Jesus had omnipotence at His disposal, though the angels had to be restrained to keep from delivering Him from death, Jesus stayed on the cross by divine appointment. The sacrifice demanded it. No wonder Isaac Watts wrote:

Well might the sun in darkness hide
And shut his glories in

When Christ, the mighty Maker, died
For man, the creature's sin.

*(Alas! And Did My Savior Bleed?)*

But did He suffer only as man, or also as God? Was the whole Trinity emotionally involved in His agony? Or was the divine nature passive, the Father accepting the payment that the Son offered on that dark day in Jerusalem?

It is unthinkable that Christ would cry, "My God, my God, why have you forsaken me?" and the Father not suffer. As parents we know that if we watched our son be crucified, he would not be the only one who would be suffering. Think of the closer relationship that exists between the members of the Trinity. Indeed, they are one in essence, one in purpose, and one in desire. If Christ suffered as man, we must boldly affirm that God suffered.

Dennis Ngien, professor at Ontario Theological Seminary and author of *The Suffering of God,* agrees that a God who cannot suffer is a God who cannot love. If God does not feel the pain of His people, it would be difficult to refute the conclusion that He is indifferent to our plight. "God suffers," says Ngien, "because He wills to love."[7] Dietrich Bonhoeffer was right when he wrote from prison, "Only a suffering God can help." Suffering is not a sign of weakness but rather entails a decision to love. If only the humanity of Christ suffered at the cross, then there was no real Incarnation. Indeed, we might conclude that only a man died on the cross, not the God-man.

George Butterick describes a picture of the Crucifixion in an Italian church with a vast and shadowy figure behind the portrait of Christ. The nail that pierces the hand of Jesus goes through to the hand of God. The spear thrust into the side of Jesus goes through into God's.[8] Bishop Stephen Neill wrote, "If the crucifixion of Jesus . . . is in some way, as Christians have believed, the dying of God himself, then . . . we can understand what God is like."[9] Luther noted that if only a man died for us, we are lost.

72

Let us say boldly that when you see Christ on the cross, you see God. There is no inconsistency between the suffering of the Messiah and the nature of God. Christ said matter-of-factly, "Anyone who has seen me has seen the Father" (John 14:9). It is simply not possible to separate Christ as man from Christ as God. "God, dying for man," wrote Pastor P. T. Forsyth, "I am not afraid of that phrase; I cannot do without it. God dying for men; and for such men—hostile, malignantly hostile men. . . . God must either inflict punishment or assume it. And He chose the latter course, as honoring the law while saving the guilty. He took His own judgment."[10]

Yet the Scriptures do stop short of saying, "God died." The reason is that immortality belongs to God's essential being: He "alone possesses immortality and dwells in unapproachable light; whom no man has seen or can see. To Him be honor and eternal dominion! Amen" (1 Tim. 6:16, NASB). So He became a *man* that He might be able to die.

Perhaps Paul's admonition to the Ephesian elders is the closest the Scriptures come to saying that God died. He said, "Be on guard for yourselves and for all the flock, among which the Holy Spirit has made you overseers, to shepherd the church of God which He purchased with *His own blood*" (Acts 20:28, NASB, emphasis mine).

Perhaps a second reason why the Bible does not say explicitly that God died is because God in the New Testament is frequently represented as "Father," and the Person who died on the cross is not the Father but the Son. But we must remember that the two persons of the Godhead can be distinguished but not separated. "Now all these things are from God, who reconciled us to Himself through Christ, and gave us the ministry of reconciliation" (2 Cor. 5:18, NASB). John Stott again urges us to remain balanced: "If we speak only of Christ suffering and dying, we overlook the initiative of the Father. If we speak only of God suffering and dying, we overlook the mediation of the Son. . . . God [was] acting in and through Christ with his whole-hearted concurrence."[11]

An embittered skeptic asked, "How could an all-knowing, all-loving God allow His Son to be murdered on a cross in order to redeem my sins? Why didn't *He* come down and go to Calvary?" The answer is, "In Christ, He did!"

Charles Wesley did not back away from the bold assertion:

> Amazing love! How can it be
> That Thou, my God, should'st die for me?
> *(And Can It Be That I Should Gain?)*

The little girl who says, "I love Jesus, but I am afraid of God," needs to have her theology corrected. If Jesus cares about her, and He does, God cares about her too. And if Christ is touched with her pain, God is touched with her pain. Let us remember that His heart cannot be separated from that of His Son. "There is only one means to endure our suffering, and that is, to understand His, to hook ours onto His, and to remember that ours is His," writes Louis Evely. Recall the woman whose son was killed in an accident, who asked her pastor angrily, "Where was your God when my son was killed?" to which he replied, "He was where He was when His Son was killed."

Our perpetual struggle is to reconcile God's love and the fact of human suffering. There are those who think that God has turned on them, that He has abandoned them in their greatest hour of need. What we want in our despair is an unveiling of the heart of God; we want to know that He not only has power, but that He also has feelings. We all have seen the pain on the face of a child when a parent remains aloof from his suffering. We can be glad that our heavenly Father is not like that; He not only knows, He feels.

If you want to see how much God is angered by the sin of the world, look at the cross. Someone has said, "There love and justice meet in one momentous catharsis of divine emotion." There was no human solution to our estrangement; how can God be just and overlook sin. How can He be love, yet punish? But God is not a man. He finds a way, one that does not compromise His justice, that does not deny His love. There at the cross we see love and justice passionately colliding and resolving themselves in mutual satisfaction.

If it was God in Christ who was murdered, if it was God who willingly allowed the forces of evil to close in on Him, then we have just uncovered another way in which Christianity differs from all other religions. Christianity says that God willingly accepted mistreatment at the hands of His creatures.

## GOD'S SUFFERING TODAY

Yes, God can suffer; yes, God did suffer. Does God still suffer?

God's suffering, I believe, did not end with the cross. He continues to feel with us in our fallenness. God does not delight in seeing us in pain, but He has hidden purposes to which He is directing all things. Remember His promise: "When you pass through the waters, I will be with you; and when you pass through the rivers, they will not sweep over you. When you walk through the fire, you will not be burned; the flames will not set you ablaze" (Isa. 43:2). The sorrows of earth are felt in heaven.

You might be acquainted with the story of Elie Wiesel, the Nobel Prize winner and Jewish survivor of the Holocaust. In the concentration camp, he was compelled to witness the hanging of two Jewish men and one Jewish boy. The two men died almost instantly, but the lad struggled for about a half-hour on the gallows.

Someone behind Wiesel muttered, "Where is God? Where is He?" That was the question that Wiesel also was asking. Then a voice within him seemed to say, "He is hanging there on the gallows."[12]

How do you interpret those words? I take them to mean that God is in the midst of mankind's suffering; God is at the receiving end of atrocities. Ravi Zacharias comments, "Where is God? Right there; in that building. Right there; in that plastic bag. The cross somehow invades us as the only reasonable point of definition for a wounded world. God is on the gallows Himself so that we might come near."[13]

Our affliction is not merely observed by a distant and only occasionally caring God but by a God who can feel our pains and hurts. Christ as our High Priest can sympathize with our weaknesses, and we can be sure that those same feelings affect our heavenly Father. To the young man who was a disciple of Christ but left the faith after his sister was brutally murdered, I say, "God cares and feels!" He is not calloused because He has observed so much evil from the beginning of the Fall. Centuries of violence and pain cannot desensitize Him—His character is unchanging and absolute.

To the woman I just spoke to on the telephone who lives with an angry, uncaring husband, I can say with integrity, "God suffers with you." God loves us with an everlasting love. If the word *love* has any meaning at all, it must mean that God feels our heartaches. "Just as a father has compassion on his children, so the LORD has compassion on those who fear Him. For He Himself knows our frame; He is mindful that we are but dust" (Ps. 103:13–14, NASB).

God is the silent sufferer; He knows, understands, and cares. He carries our sorrows close to His heart. When Christ asked Saul, who at the time was imprisoning Christians, "Saul, Saul, why do you persecute me?" (Acts 9:4), He implied that He Himself felt the blows and the pangs of injustice. And since the members of the Godhead are one, I'm sure the Father felt them too.

In Africa a fire ravaged a hut, burning quickly and intensely, killing all in a family—except one. A stranger ran into the burning house and snatched a small boy from the flames, carried him to safety, and disappeared in the darkness.

The next day the tribe met to decide what should be done with the lad. Perhaps superstitiously, they assumed he must be a special child since he survived the fire. A man known for his wisdom insisted that he adopt the boy; another known for his wealth thought he was the best qualified.

As the discussion ensued, a young, unknown man walked into the middle of the circle and insisted that he had prior claim to the child.

Then he showed them his hands, freshly burned in the fire of the past night. He was the rescuer and therefore insisted that the child was rightfully his.

So our scarred Savior claims us. Bonhoeffer was right: only a suffering God can help. Only a suffering God can redeem.

> The other gods were strong; but Thou wast weak
> They rode, but Thou didst stumble to a throne;
> But to our wounds only God's wounds can speak
> And not a god has wounds but Thou alone.[14]

We have not solved the mystery of suffering. We have only said that we can endure it much better when we know that the Father and Son are for us; they have personally tasted the grief that confronts us in a sinful world.

This does not mean that we have all of our questions answered, but we do have in the cross the clearest proof that God cares. Our comfort lies in the fact that our God not only walks with us, He feels our sorrows and distresses. And someday His people will more fully understand.

In the next chapter we shall consider an entirely different aspect of God's purposes. We will discover that although God does suffer, He has also limited the gift of salvation to those who put faith in his Son. If we think that God's compassion will outweigh His justice, or if we think that His primary goal is the happiness of His creation, we are mistaken. We will contemplate the exceedingly complex purposes of God.

## A PERSONAL RESPONSE

Let me suggest that you read Hosea 11 and try to grasp the deeply felt love of God, His anger and sense of betrayal, but also His delight when his wayward children are reconciled. Here we have the yearning of God and his disappointment vividly described. Worship God by reading the text, trying to connect with the emotions described. A few of the verses are printed below; it would be better for you to read the entire chapter in your own Bible.

> When Israel was a child, I loved him,
>> and out of Egypt I called my son.
> But the more I called Israel,
>> the further they went from me.
> They sacrificed to the Baals
>> and they burned incense to images.
> It was I who taught Ephraim to walk,
>> taking them by the arms;
> but they did not realize
>> it was I who healed them.
> I led them with cords of human kindness, with ties of love.
>
> . . . How can I give you up, Ephraim?
>> How can I hand you over, Israel?
> How can I treat you like Admah?
>> How can I make you like Zeboiim?
> My heart is changed within me;
>> all my compassion is aroused.
> I will not carry out my fierce anger,
>> nor will I turn and devastate Ephraim.
> For I am God, and not man—
>> the Holy One among you.
>> I will not come in wrath.
>
> (Hos. 11:1–4, 8–9)

We can be grateful that our God can identify with the hurts of His creation.

**LIE 5** # God Is Obligated to Save Followers of Other Religions

VISUALIZE A MOTHER in a Third World country, living in squalor. Her husband has been killed in a civil war. Her daughter has been brutally raped. The mother trudges dozens of miles to get a few cups of milk for her starving children. An epidemic sweeps through her village, she is infected, and after months of unbelievable suffering, she dies. And, because she belonged to a non-Christian religion, according to Christian theology, she goes from one hell to another. She exchanges a temporal hell for an eternal one.

Is such a scenario thinkable? Does it not raise serious questions about the love and justice of God? If, as we have learned in the last chapter, God has emotions and suffers with us, isn't it inconceivable that some of the people He created would be in an eternal hell? And, to make the matter more difficult, many who experience this eternal lostness would not have had even an opportunity to believe in Christ. Is it not hopelessly arrogant to suggest that there is one way to heaven and those who miss it through no fault of their own will be lost forever?

Needless to say, this topic generates heated controversy. A *Chicago Tribune* article "Theologians Opening Heaven's Gate a Bit Wider" says that both Catholic and Protestant theologians are denouncing the outdated notion that eternal salvation is limited to those who believe in Christ.[1] The cultural pressure of pluralism and the growing presence of people from other religions make the exclusivistic view almost impossible to maintain. There are good and bad people in all religions. If God really does love the whole world, He could not possibly limit salvation to those who were fortunate enough to be born in the West, to those who could easily hear about Christ—could He? The thought that He would condemn some to everlasting perdition because of an accident of birth is too much to believe.

We have all wished that the way to heaven were broader so that we could give a more acceptable reply to those who ridicule the Christian faith because, in their way of thinking, it does not take into account sincere worshipers in other religions. How do we answer those who accuse us of heartless narrow-mindedness? Or those who say that their God, thankfully, is more broad-minded than ours?

Yes, I can hear the objections: "What about those who have never heard of Christ—are they excluded from God's grace?"

"Is it fair for God to send anyone to hell, especially those who never had a chance to believe the message?"

"Is it possible for sincere believers of other religions to be saved through Christ though they will not know Him until they get to heaven?"

"Are not Christians bigoted to believe in the superiority of Christianity?"

These are not theoretical questions: they are matters of life and death, of heaven and hell. Missionaries tell us that when people from other religions come to believe in Christ they often ask, "What is the final destiny of our parents who died believing in a different religion?" And as we become personally acquainted with those of other religions, the question of their salvation is never far from our minds.

Where can we turn for answers to these questions? Who can arbitrate between competing viewpoints? Should we look within ourselves for the answer? Should we look to nature, or simply take a consensus of opinions? Does what *we* think really matter? John Stott writes:

> If we come to the Scriptures with our minds made up, expecting to
> hear from it only an echo of our own thoughts and never the thunder-

clap of God's, then indeed he will not speak to us and we shall only be confirmed in our own prejudices. We must allow the Word of God to confront us, to disturb our security, to undermine our complacency and to overthrow our patterns of thought and behavior.[2]

Once again we must not form our conception of God "from the bottom up" but humbly submit to God's Word. We believe in a self-revealing God who has given us a shaft of light, a glimmer of His purposes. As we move through this chapter, we will begin with what is clear in the Bible and move to that which is more obscure. We will answer four questions that lead us to the heart of these sensitive matters.

## IS SALVATION THROUGH CHRIST ALONE?

We've already learned that the Bible is very clear: salvation is available only through Christ. To quote Jesus' own words, "I am the way and the truth and the life. No one comes to the Father except through me" (John 14:6). Paul the apostle put it this way: "For there is one God and one mediator between God and men, the man Christ Jesus, who gave himself as a ransom for all men—the testimony given in its proper time" (1 Tim. 2:5–6). The apostles agreed, and Peter stated: "Salvation is found in no one else, for there is no other name under heaven given to men by which we must be saved" (Acts 4:12).

We've reviewed compelling reasons why Christ is not just one option among others. He is not just a teacher as are the founders of other religions; Jesus is a Savior. Only He is qualified to bring people to God. Keep in mind that we have to be perfect for God to accept us, and Christ is the only One who can forgive us and credit us with the perfection we need.

The Old Testament believers were saved on credit. God "overlooked" their sins for the time being, until Christ came and made a payment God could accept. Just as you can enjoy a new car and pay for it later, so the families of Abraham, Isaac, and Jacob enjoyed benefits that would be purchased later. So they have the same mediator, the same sacrifice as we.

These facts in themselves do not settle the question of whether other religions can be the doorway to Christ. When asked, "Is it possible that people who follow other religions will also be saved because of Christ?" some theologians suggest that the answer is *yes*. These teachers see other religions as friendly competitors who have much in common with Christianity and the work of the *Logos* (Christ), who enlightens every man that comes into the world. Clark Pinnock in his book *A Wideness in God's Mercy* and John Sanders in *No Other Name* insist that Christ is the only way of salvation, but it is not necessary to place direct faith in Him in order to benefit from His work on the cross and resurrection. God, their argument goes, knows that Christ is the only way of salvation, but those who have not heard the gospel are ignorant of this. Their own religion might function as a "schoolmaster" that unwittingly leads them to Christ.

Pinnock and Sanders would agree with Raymond Panikkar that the "good and bona fide Hindu is saved by Christ and not by Hinduism, but it is through the sacraments of Hinduism, through the message of morality and the good life, through the mysterion that comes down to him through Hinduism that Christ saves the Hindus normally."[3] Panikkar concludes that people can indeed be saved by Christ through the channel of other religions.

Various theologians have made suggestions to explain how God brings the sincere devotees of other religions to salvation. First, there is the "later light" view, taken from this passage in 1 Peter: "For Christ died for sins once for all, the righteous for the unrighteous, to bring you to God. He was put to death in the body but made alive by the Spirit, through whom also he went and preached to the spirits in prison who disobeyed long ago when God waited patiently in the days of Noah while the ark was being built" (3:18–20).

Some interpret this passage to mean that Christ preached the gospel to those who were in Hades. They conclude that people will get an opportunity to accept or reject Christ after death. In the early church, Irenaeus and Tertullian taught that Jesus delivered only the believers of the Old Testament from hell when He descended there; Clement of Alexandria and Athanasius taught that Jesus delivered both Jews and Gentiles from hell and that this form of evangelism still continues today.

But there are serious objections to this view. For one thing, it is by no means certain that Peter taught that Christ went to Hades at all. Perhaps he means that by the same Holy Spirit, Christ through Noah preached to spirits who are now in prison; these spirits would be human beings who lived during the time of Noah. But even if we grant that Christ went and preached to these spirits in between His death and resurrection, we have no idea what He said. Perhaps He only announced His triumph or explained the reason for their just judgment. There is no evidence that He gave them a final opportunity to repent. Finally, it is stretching the text to the breaking point to assume that Christ is doing the same today. Regardless of what interpretation we accept, the passage refers to an event that is past without the slightest hint that it continues.

A second suggestion says God will save people who don't accept Christ as Savior based on His foreknowledge. Since He knows not only what has happened but also what would have happened under different circumstances, he would know whether someone who didn't hear the gospel in, say, Sri Lanka would have accepted it if he had been born in Canada. On this basis, the argument goes, He redeems them.

But even if election were based on foreknowledge (a view I don't accept), the idea that God saves some because of what would have been the case under different circumstances is wholly conjecture. Christ said that if He had performed His miracles in Tyre and Sidon rather than in faithless cities, "they would have repented long ago in sackcloth and ashes" (Matt. 11:21). Yet He gave no hint that this means that Tyre and Sidon will be saved in future judgment. We can all think of circumstances in which, to our mind at least, virtually anyone would accept Christ. But the Bible teaches that God takes into account what has happened rather than what might have happened.

Third, there are those who believe that God simply makes an exception and chooses to accept Christ's sacrifice on behalf of sincere individuals of other religions. In other words, He credits their sin to Christ's account even though they do not know this to be the case—though eventually they will. God, we are told, made such exceptions for Enoch, Job, Melchizedek, Jethro, and others in the Old Testament. The Savior, then, accepts the sincere Hindu or Buddhist who meets Christ only at death. Just like children, who many believe are saved without personal faith in Christ, others from diverse religions are saved though they have not explicitly believed in Him.

This argument is unconvincing, however, because there is good reason to believe that the men of the Old Testament I referred to above responded because they had special revelation; they were told about Jehovah; they were not saved while following some other god. As for the analogy regarding infants, they do not have the ability to respond to even the general revelation of nature or conscience, so their situation is entirely different. There is a difference between those who cannot hear (infants) and those who are old enough to hear and understand if the opportunity were afforded them.

Many cite Cornelius as an example of someone who was converted without direct faith in Christ. He was a devout man who feared God with all his household. Peter, you will recall, received a vision that corresponded with one Cornelius received. When they met and Peter realized that God intended to save this man, he said, "I most certainly understand now that God is not one to show partiality, but in every nation the man who fears Him and does what is right, is welcome to Him" (Acts 10:34–35, NASB).

Should we interpret this, as some do, that God accepts those who fear Him, no matter what their religion? John Sanders writes, "Cornelius was already a saved believer before Peter arrived, but he was not a Christian believer."[4] From this he concludes that some people are saved though they are not Christians.

Again this interpretation appears flawed. For one thing, as Gary

Phillips points out in an article entitled "Evangelical Pluralism: A Singular Problem," New Testament God-fearers believed in the truth of propitiatory sacrifice, and Cornelius had already responded to special revelation (Acts 10:3–8).[5] For another, the text says that he was not saved until Peter preached the Word to him (Acts 11:14). Finally, and most important, we must interpret Peter's remark in light of the context: he had just experienced a vision convincing him that Gentiles are also included in the plan of salvation. When he says that God does not show partiality but accepts other God-fearers, he is not saying that they are saved independently of the gospel. He is simply stating what to him was a radical idea; namely, that anyone, even Gentiles, could respond to the message of redemption.

There are those who would disagree with Pinnock in some respects and agree with him in others. But both he and Sanders use a principle of interpretation that almost certainly guarantees the outcome of what they are looking for. It is that man's idea of fairness should largely control what we believe regarding the fate of those who do not know Christ as Savior.

It is lamentable, I think, that Sanders would say that God must have some special arrangement for the unevangelized, and if not, He would be less worthy of worship, less just, and less loving than humans.[6] Obviously by this criteria God should not allow earthquakes, famines, and wars, since any sensitive human being would prevent such atrocities if it were within his power. This is bad reasoning and bad theology.

It is dangerous to use our understanding of fairness to control the outcome of our biblical interpretations. Gary Phillips is right when he comments:

Once fairness is used as a criterion (and exceptions inevitably tend to proliferate), other inequities besides ignorance vie for attention: some may have heard the gospel from a parent who abused them, or from a pastor who later committed adultery. Others may be told about Christ from someone whose intellectual abilities did not commend

Christianity as a faith for thoughtful people. Still others are unfortunate enough to have wealth—a tremendous hindrance to salvation.... All of these, through no fault of their own, would be negatively disposed toward the gospel.[7]

The point is clear: every human being can reason that he/she rejected the gospel because something or someone was "unfair." We'd all like to rewrite what the Bible says about God to make Him fair. We've all thought of what we would do if we were God to minimize the suffering of human beings in this life and in the one to come. The problem, of course, is that we are not God.

Clark Pinnock's theological pilgrimage is useful in understanding his bent toward a "fair" (by his definition) God. Years ago he abandoned Calvinism, with its emphasis on God's sovereign choice in salvation, in favor of Arminianism, with its emphasis on free will. Then he moved further downstream from traditional Arminianism and opted for a belief in a finite God, a God who does not even know the future. He argued that if God knows who will be saved and who will be lost, the future is in some sense fixed. Thus Pinnock's God does not choose people even on the basis of foreknowledge; indeed He does not choose anyone, but rather we choose Him because His knowledge is limited. He does not even know who will be saved and who will be lost!

Pinnock thinks that God took a risk when He created the world and gave men free will. He further concludes that God does not know the decisions of free men in advance: "Genuine novelty can appear in history which cannot even be predicted by God."[8] This ignorance on God's part, Pinnock believes, makes the gospel appear more credible, more "fair." (I will consider this view in detail in the chapter #7.)

Pinnock's theories do not end there. Once he decided that God had to be "fair," he adopted the view that those who are sincere in other religions can be saved without faith in Christ. And if they are not saved in this life, they can ask for mercy in the life to come. Anyone who stands before God in judgment and asks for mercy will receive it. God's books, we are told, are never closed. And if there are still some wicked left who have not availed themselves of all these opportunities, fairness requires that they be annihilated rather than consciously suffer forever.[9]

With that in mind we should not be surprised that he writes:

> When we approach the man of a faith other than our own, it will be in a spirit of expectancy to find how God has been speaking to him and what new understanding of the grace and love of God we may ourselves discover in this encounter. Our first task in approaching another people, another culture, another religion is to take off the shoes, for the place we are approaching is holy. Else we find ourselves treading on men's dreams. More seriously still, we may forget that God was here before our arrival.[10]

Pinnock sees others' religions as transitional, and thus Christians have opportunities to aid them in seeking truth through dialogue. "God the Logos has more going on by way of redemption than what happened in first-century Palestine," he writes.[11] Incredibly, Pinnock appears to believe in a universal *Logos* who is at work in all religions.

Our human idea of fairness is based on a limited understanding of God's purposes; God may have a different agenda. Isaiah put it this way:

> "For My thoughts are not your thoughts,
> Neither are your ways My ways," declares the LORD.
> "For as the heavens are higher than the earth,
> So are My ways higher than your ways,
> And My thoughts than your thoughts."
>
> (Isa. 55:8–9, NASB)

Gary Phillips says accurately, "Speculations are often rather suddenly taught as certainties; a remote interpretation of a text is taken as the real interpretation." Once a theologian like Pinnock and a professor like Sanders interpret a passage to fit their view, they use it is as a grid to reinterpret dozens of other passages that contradict their viewpoint. We have no right to be more broad-minded than God. To quote Gary Phillips once more, we "would rather err on the side of safety than gamble on speculative leniency."[12] We cannot go beyond what God has revealed. If He has a plan to save those of other religions, He has not seen fit to reveal it to us.

## HOW DOES THE BIBLE VIEW
## NON-CHRISTIAN RELIGIONS?

The Scriptures require us to view other religions as the flawed attempts of man to reach God through human effort and insight. Paul made two points about paganism. First, he said that those who worship idols actually are worshiping demons: "The things which the Gentiles sacrifice, they sacrifice to demons, and not to God; and I do not want you to become sharers in demons. You cannot drink the cup of the Lord and the cup of demons; you cannot partake of the table of the Lord and the table of demons" (1 Cor. 10:20–21, NASB).

He did not say that the Gentiles (pagans) were really worshiping God in their own way. Either we worship the true God, or we worship idols. Read these passages from the Old Testament and make your own conclusions:

You shall tear down their altars and smash their sacred pillars and burn their Asherim with fire, and you shall cut down the engraved images of their gods, and you shall obliterate their name from that place.

(Deut. 12:3, NASB)

For all the gods of the peoples are idols,
But the LORD made the heavens.

(Ps. 96:5, NASB)

> Then Elijah commanded them, "Seize the prophets of Baal. Don't let anyone get away!" They seized them, and Elijah had them brought down to the Kishon Valley and slaughtered there.
>
> (1 Kings 18:40)

Second, Paul taught that religions evolved because man did not honor the true God. Because of rebellion, they "exchanged the glory of the incorruptible God for an image in the form of corruptible man and of birds and four-footed animals and crawling creatures" (Rom. 1:23, NASB). One characteristic of idolatry is that it always confuses the creature with the Creator. Satan orchestrated false religions, offering a smorgasbord of options, but all of them stand against the gospel of Christ.

There is a story about the blind men of Indostan who investigated an elephant, and each came to a different conclusion as to how the beast should be described. The man who had the tail thought it was a rope, the man who embraced a leg thought it felt like a tree, and the man who held the trunk thought it was a snake. Some make the point that different religions are simply different aspects of the same reality. But if we reflect on what the Bible says about other religions, we will have to conclude that we are not even describing the same elephant!

Even those who seek the true God cannot come to any saving knowledge of the Almighty without the light of revelation. On Mars Hill, Paul said that God determined the appointed times of the nations of the earth and their boundaries "that they [mankind] should seek God, if perhaps they might grope for Him and find Him, though He is not far from each one of us" (Acts 17:27, NASB). Then he urged his listeners to believe in the God who raised Christ from the dead. Without the light of revelation, the best man could do is to "grope" for understanding, straining for a hint of hope and means of forgiveness.

I do not deny that there might be some good ethical teaching in other religions. Buddhism, in particular, stresses a form of selfless devotion that appears to have something in common with Christianity. We should expect this, since all people are created in the image of God and have a moral consciousness. But it is not necessary for a religion to be totally false in order for it to be disastrously wrong. Other religions fail at the most central point—namely, the question of how sinners can be reconciled to God. In the end, if they worship at all, they worship another god.

Regardless of how much we want to see non-Christians saved, we must be cautious about being more lenient than biblical teaching allows. We must bow before God as He is and not as the God we, given our finite understanding, would want Him to be.

## HOW WILL THOSE WHO HAVE NOT HEARD OF CHRIST BE JUDGED?

What we want to know is how God can be just if He does not accept people who have not heard the gospel. We wonder if His love would not accept others as they are, whether they accept His Son or not. The biblical answer is that God will judge people by what they did with what they knew. In other words, He will judge those who have never heard the gospel on the basis of *general revelation*.

General revelation, includes, first, the light of nature. Scripture tells us:

> The wrath of God is being revealed from heaven against all the godlessness and wickedness of men who suppress the truth by their wickedness, since what may be known about God is plain to them, because God has made it plain to them. For since the creation of the world God's invisible qualities—his eternal power and divine nature—have been clearly seen, being understood from what has been made, so that men are without excuse.
>
> For although they knew God, they neither glorified him as God nor gave thanks to him, but their thinking became futile and their foolish hearts were darkened.
>
> (Rom. 1:18–21)

God displays His eternal power and divine nature clearly in creation. Even as God who cannot be seen became visible in Jesus, the God who cannot be seen is visible in His creation.

There is a second form of general revelation, and that is the God-consciousness that exists in every human being. Every person carries an innate sense of right and wrong, of transcendent values, a knowledge that there is a standard of righteous behavior. Our own hearts tell us the truth of this:

> For all who have sinned without the Law will also perish without the Law; and all who have sinned under the Law will be judged by the Law. . . . For when Gentiles who do not have the Law do instinctively the things of the Law, these, not having the Law, are a law to themselves, in that they show the work of the Law written in their hearts, their conscience bearing witness, and their thoughts alternately accusing or else defending them.
>
> (Rom. 2:12, 14–15, NASB)

Even the Gentiles, who did not have the law revealed on Sinai, do "instinctively" the things of the law. So God will judge them on the basis of conscience and nature; they did not receive the Ten Commandments, but they do have rudimentary moral law written in their hearts. God would not expect them to keep the Sabbath day holy, since such instruction can come only through special revelation. But they know murder and theft are wrong; they know that selfishness is wrong. So the question will be, how well did they live up to these expectations?

God will not ask those who have never heard of Christ why they did not accept Him! That would be unjust. Judgment is always according to knowledge, according to the light given. As F. F. Bruce said, God will judge non-Christians "by the light that is available, not by the light that is unavailable." Paul argues, however, that both the Gentiles and Jews will be found "without excuse" in the day of judgment.

What will this judgment reveal? First, it will show that no one lives up to the light he knows. Paul says the Gentiles "suppress" the truth by their wickedness. Left to ourselves, we deaden the conscience and we reinterpret nature to suit our desires. In the end we are all dishonest creatures who deceive ourselves, fool others, and ultimately try to lie to God. We are all basically dishonest.

Second, this judgment will confirm that nature cannot give us what we need, namely the righteousness of God credited to our account. If God's standards for acceptance were not His own holiness, if He could accept human imperfection, there would be hope, but He cannot. No Jew has ever lived up to the law of Moses, and no Gentile has ever lived up to the light of conscience. The verdict of God is clear: "All have sinned and fall short of the glory of God" (Rom. 3:23, NASB). Thus only Christ will do; only He can give us the perfect righteousness we need.

I believe as well that those who are willing to admit that they fall short,  those who turn from man-made gods and desire the one true God, are given additional light so that they can be led to the knowledge of Christ. As God works in people's hearts, some move to honestly seek Him. My belief is consistent with Paul's words to the Athenians that we read earlier. God, he said, determined where the different nations would be geographically, and He "did this so that men would seek him and perhaps reach out for him and find him, though he is not far from each one of us. 'For in him we live and move and have our being'" (Acts 17:27–28).

More than a few people who were reared in non-Christian religions tell us that when they turned from their own gods to seek the "one true God," they had a dream about Jesus and later came in contact with a messenger of the gospel. Or, though there might not have been a dream, through some providential happenstance they came in contact with the New Testament.

I must caution, however, that though such stories are enlightening, they do not provide a basis for a final theological position on the issue. We must humbly leave the final verdict to God, acknowledging that there is much about God's relationship with those of other religions that we do not know. We are left only with the biblical principle that God bases His judgment on knowledge, and God will take into account the response and behavior of each person.

## WHAT ABOUT THE FINAL JUDGMENT?

When God judges, He will do so according to meticulous standards of evidence and justice. Those who come under the protection and salvation of Christ will be saved, for Christ has borne their debt; those who have responded only to general revelation will have to bear the consequences of their own deeds. But by no means will the punishment be the same for everyone. Listen to the words of Christ:

> That servant who knows his master's will and does not get ready or does not do what his master wants will be beaten with many blows. But the one who does not know and does things deserving punishment will be beaten with few blows. From everyone who has been given much, much will be demanded; and from the one who has been entrusted with much, much more will be asked.
>
> (Luke 12:47–48)

General revelation is a basis for judgment, but not for salvation. If you need one thousand dollars for college and I give you only one hundred dollars, my gift is not enough to get you into college, but it is enough to judge your response. With this one hundred dollars I can tell whether you love me or spurn me. And how you respond may determine whether or not you ever receive the full amount.

We can be sure that first, there will be degrees of punishment commensurate with knowledge; and second, that God will take into account every bit of information about the circumstance and inner heart response. God's knowledge will be detailed, balanced, and complete.

God will distribute justice so accurately, with such perfect balance, that throughout eternity we will sing, "Righteous and true are Thy ways" (Rev. 15:3, NASB). I believe that even those who are lost—yes, even the devil himself—will have to confess for all of eternity that what God did was just and right. God never commits an injustice.

Is God obligated to save everyone? Strictly speaking, He is under no obligation to save anyone. He is, however, required to be just. It is unthinkable that the God who tells us to act justly should Himself not be just. And yes, He is obligated to be loving because He commands us to love. His love is a just love; His mercy is just mercy. God, so far as we know, has chosen not to save any of the fallen angels. He has consigned them to judgment without mercy. He has judged them solely for what they did in light of His revelation, just as He judges those who know only general revelation without seeking the true God.

Is God fair? That is a loaded question. We've already mentioned the danger of bringing to the Word our own notions of what fairness is. If we think that fairness means that God must treat everyone alike, then be assured, God is not "fair" in that sense of the word. An earthquake in Turkey kills fifteen thousand people; a mud slide in Venezuela kills thirty thousand. In the midwestern United States where I live, there has never been a serious earthquake in, say, the last fifty years. God does not treat nations or areas of the world alike. Is that fair? (In the next chapter we shall study how God relates to natural disasters.)

God did not treat Hammurabi, the king of Babylon, like He did Abraham. No, God is under no obligation to treat everyone alike. We have a world of people who have unequal abilities, unequal opportunities, and unequal life spans. In some God displays His mercy, in others His justice. This is simply the way God has chosen to run His world. He can do this and be fair. I cannot emphasize too strongly that we cannot stand in judgment of God on this issue; we can simply bow and accept His authority and the hiddenness of His purposes.

Carl Henry, responding to those who wish to make the gate to heaven broader than it is in the New Testament, is right when he says, "The modern misjudgment of God flows easily from contemporary theology's preoccupation with love as the core of God's being, while righteousness is subordinated and denied equal ultimacy with love in the nature of the deity."[13]

There is no standard independent of God by which mankind can judge the Almighty. God does not have to conform to our standard of fairness, though He must be fair in keeping with His nature and long-range objectives. Within these parameters, He is free to do as He pleases. If we say, as some do, that it would be unfair for God to require eternal punishment for sins committed over a relatively short period of a few years, we can do no better than to quote the words of Jonathan Edwards:

> Our obligation to love, honor and obey any being is in proportion to his loveliness, honorableness and authority. . . . But God is a being infinitely lovely, because he hath infinite excellency and beauty. . . . So a sin against God, being a violation of infinite obligations, must be a crime infinitely heinous, and so deserving infinite punishment. . . . The eternity of the punishment of the ungodly men renders it infinite . . . and therefore renders it no more than proportionate to the heinousness of what they are guilty of.[14]

John Piper points out that the everlasting horrors of hell are a vivid demonstration of the everlasting value of the glory of God that sinners belittle. Infinite punishment rests on those who are infinitely guilty. Paul asked, "What shall we say then? There is no injustice with God, is there? May it never be!" (Rom. 9:14, NASB). Yes, even if we were lost, God would be fair.

Paul continued the argument that God displays His justice and wrath in His dealings with the ungodly but gives His mercy and grace to those who believe. When Paul speaks of God's impartiality (Rom. 2:11), he means simply that God will judge the unbelieving world by the principle we have already stated, namely, knowledge and performance.

Is it not dangerous, or possibly even presumptuous, to insist that God conform to our thinking or else we will withhold our unreserved adoration? In a movie called *Rudy,* I'm told, a professor of Notre Dame is speaking to a football player who is critical of the fact that he was rejected from the squad. The professor says that after years of teaching he has come to two propositions that are incontrovertibly true: "There is a God, and I'm not Him!" Two lessons worth learning!

The fact that God does not owe salvation to everyone (indeed, He does not owe it to anyone) still troubles us because we ask, "Would not a loving God have arranged the world in such a way that more people could have taken advantage of Christ's supreme work?" Love, one would think, would have even overcome any barriers that exist to the salvation of all men.

However, God has a bigger plan than we can see; He has an eternal purpose that inspired Him to choose this world and its arrangements. The theologian Benjamin Warfield points out that the love of God must of necessity be under the control of His righteousness and His eternal purposes. When asked why God does not save more people, he replies that the old answer is the only sufficient one: "God in his love saves as many of the guilty race of man as he can get the consent of his whole nature to save."[15] In our contemplations of these things, we must take into account God's eternal and mysterious objectives. "The secret things belong to the LORD our God, but the things revealed belong to us and to our sons forever, that we may observe all the words of this law" (Deut. 29:29, NASB).

If God has a plan to save men and women without personal faith in Christ, He has chosen not to reveal it. We must resist the temptation to make the Scriptures say what we think they should. Our role is to spread the gospel with the firm conviction that faith comes by hearing and people cannot believe what they do not know.

## CHALLENGING CONCLUSIONS

We must conclude, then, that the need to proclaim the gospel is urgent. We must keep in mind that God's purposes in the world are transnational; His intention to have representatives in heaven from every tribe, tongue, and people will be fulfilled. When Jesus commanded, "Go into all the world and preach the gospel" (Mark 16:15, NASB). He confirmed that He is the Savior of the *world,* not just the Savior for those within His hearing. In some parts of Africa, multitudes are being converted!

My second conclusion is this: I would rather die as a person who never heard of Christ than as a person who heard the gospel and rejected it. Yes, I would rather die as the distraught mother I referred to at the beginning of this chapter than to have heard of Christ but rejected Him—perhaps because His exclusive claims offended me.

My experience is that most people who are worried about the fate of people of other religions are not sufficiently concerned about themselves. But if those who know only general revelation are "without excuse," how much more are those who have held a Bible in their hands, those who have some acquaintance with a Christian church, and those who could, if they desired, seek Christ as their Savior?

Are Christians arrogant to believe that theirs is the only way? Of course, it is not "our way," as if this is what we came up with! On a talk show, a rabbi accused a Christian of claiming to do God's work for Him: "Christians," he said, "open heaven's gates for some and not for others." But of course, it is God alone who opens heaven's gates for whom He wishes and closes them for whom He wishes. All we can do is read the Bible to find out what He has said about the matter. The Scriptures teach that the narrow way is "God's way," and we are given the privilege of believing it. That we should be privileged to put our faith in Christ humbles us and is, in fact, the perfect remedy for arrogance.

## A PERSONAL RESPONSE

This is one of several difficult chapters in this book. There are, perhaps, three possible responses to what God has revealed. First, some who hear these hard sayings might be tempted to drift toward *agnosticism:* they would say that the idea of conscious, eternal punishment is too difficult to accept even for those who have rejected the gospel, and much more incredible for those who haven't. A second possibility is *anger:* if this is the way God runs His world, I will defy Him. Like the man who told me, "If I go to hell, I will curse God for all of eternity. It is a matter of honor."

Another possibility is *awe:* the overwhelming sense that if this is what God has revealed, we must accept it with humility. God has not answered all of our questions, but He reminds us that He is God, and our responsibility is to worship Him. Let us humbly acknowledge the words of Scripture:

> Woe to him who quarrels with his Maker,
>> to him who is but a potsherd among the potsherds on the ground.
>
> Does the clay say to the potter,
>> "What are you making?"
>
> Does your work say,
>> "He has no hands"?
>
> (Isa. 45:9)

> What then shall we say? Is God unjust? Not at all. For he says to Moses,
> "I will have mercy on whom I have mercy,
>> and I will have compassion on whom I have compassion."
>
> (Rom. 9:14–15)

If you desire, say this prayer with me: "Lord, we accept Your verdict; we acknowledge Your right to do that which is pleasing in Your sight. Help us to rejoice in what You have revealed and leave to You the mysteries of Your will. Help us to remember: You are the potter; we are the clay. We believe You do all things well. Amen."

# LIE 6 | God Takes No Responsibility for Natural Disasters

I'M TOLD THAT AFTER AN EARTHQUAKE in California some years ago, a group of ministers met for a prayer breakfast. As they discussed the shifting expressways and ruined buildings, they agreed that for all practical purposes, God had nothing to do with this disaster. The earth is fallen, so earthquakes just happen according to certain laws of the natural order. Yet surprisingly, when one of the ministers closed in prayer, he thanked God for the timing of the earthquake that came at five o'clock in the morning, when there were few cars on the expressways and the sidewalks were largely empty. And when he finished the prayer, his colleagues chimed in with a hearty "Amen."

So, did God have anything to do with that earthquake or didn't He? Why should anyone thank God for the timing of the earthquake if He was but a neutral force regarding its occurrence? Or why should we ever pray that we would be delivered out of such a calamity if God is not directly connected to what is happening in this fallen world?

"No, God! No, God! No, God!" These are the words of a man who apparently thought God had something to do with nature; he prayed as he hid in his basement while a killer tornado destroyed his home and business. Hundreds of homeless families roamed through rubble when dozens of furious tornadoes ripped through miles of Oklahoma and parts of Kansas, killing at least forty-three people and destroying more than 1,500 homes and hundreds of businesses. One huge funnel cloud skipped across the ground for four hours and was classified 5-F, the most powerful tornado there is with winds of more than 250 miles per hour.[1]

Statistics in themselves are quite meaningless. But think of the two-year-old child ripped from his father's hands, thrown dozens of feet into the air, then slammed against the ground. Or the father who crawled into a tornado shelter only to drown when it filled with water.[2]

All this was minor in comparison to the 1999 earthquake in Turkey, which killed fifteen thousand people. Just read this account filed by a journalist, which helps us visualize and feel the agony of the families left behind.

> The choice is between two types of hell: the one where you lie in sodden blankets in a muddy field or forest floor in the rain, or the one where you find any shelter on the pavements of the cities and sleep among the ruins where the rats are flourishing and the dead still lie in their thousands.
>
> The lost people of this devastated 200-mile industrialized corridor of northwestern Turkey have made their choice. They are going into the hills in increasing numbers. Terrified and traumatized to the point where they can barely feel and cry for those who have died, they have only one thought—to get away from these obscene places they once called home.
>
> As each hour passes, what were once bustling towns are being emptied as more than 250,000 people accept that life there is no longer possible. So great is the damage that four major towns . . . have to be razed. Not a single house in a chain of communities stretching from Istanbul to Adapazari is safe to occupy.
>
> Yesterday it again rained without stopping. Those still remaining here covered themselves in black bin-liners and sheets, and either wandered like black and white ghosts, or tried to sleep wherever they could.[3]

I think of the tidal waves in Honduras, which killed about twenty-five thousand people and left perhaps a half million homeless. Mud slides in Venezuela killed an estimated fifty thousand in just a few days. On television we see the poverty, the orphans, the dirty water, and the devastated cities. We are not able to comprehend the magnitude of the disaster. Thanks to the news media, we hear and see the pictures, but a few days later, the news bulletins subside yet the distraught people, bless them, live with the tragedies for the rest of their lives.

Many people refer to these events as "acts of God," while others think it necessary to absolve God of any personal involvement. They insist that He is an interested observer, having committed the world of nature to its fate; He sees these terrifying events with minimal involvement. Yes, He could prevent them, but He has chosen a "hands-off" policy, only occasionally interfering with natural laws.

The purpose of this chapter is to answer five questions: Is God in control of natural disasters or not? If the answer is yes, when we fight nature, do we fight God? If so, dare we charge God with doing evil? How shall we interpret these events, and what messages is God trying to send us through such devastation? And finally, can a God who allows (plans?) such horrific disasters be trusted?

## IS GOD IN CONTROL OF NATURAL DISASTERS?

That nature is fallen is clear from Scriptures. God told Adam, "Cursed is the ground because of you; through painful toil you will eat of it all the days of your life. It will produce thorns and thistles for you, and you will eat the plants of the field" (Gen. 3:17–18). Somewhere I heard a story about a man who spent a great deal of his time beautifying the landscape and tending a flower garden. A friend stopped by, admired the sight, and said, "My, what a wonder God created here!" The gardener replied, "Well, yes, but you should have seen what it looked like when God had it by Himself!" Yes, if we want beauty and symmetry, we must tend the garden.

When God cursed man, He also cursed nature. God would not allow sinful man to continue to live in a sinless paradise. And just as we have our good side and dark side, so, too, does nature. Now nature awaits our redemption so that it can be redeemed along with us. Thankfully, the curse will be reversed, as Paul confirmed: "The creation waits in eager expectation for the sons of God to be revealed. For the creation was subjected to frustration, not by its own choice, but by the will of the one who subjected it, in hope that the creation itself will be liberated from its bondage to decay and brought into the glorious freedom of the children of God" (Rom. 8:19–21).

Every day we see the result of the curse: tidal waves, earthquakes, tornadoes, hurricanes, drought, and floods. In fact, the number of natural disasters is on the increase, with multiplied thousands killed each year in the powerful upheavals of natural forces. Does this mean that God has removed Himself from nature? Does He really have a "hands - off" policy when it comes to these tragedies?

We must distinguish between the immediate cause of these events and their ultimate cause. The immediate cause of an earthquake is a fault beneath the earth's crust; specifically, the top of the earth's crust moves in one direction; the lower level gradually moves in the opposite direction. The immediate cause of a tornado is wind and temperature patterns, yet the ultimate cause of these events is God. He rules nature either directly or through secondary causes, but either way, He is in charge. After all, He is the Creator, the sustainer of all things. We sing with Isaac Watts:

> There's not a plant or flower below,
> But makes Thy glories known;
> And clouds arise, and tempests blow,
> By order from Thy throne.
> (*I Sing the Mighty Power of God*)

Generations ago when radio was invented, I'm told that some Christians explained that the near-miraculous transmission of the human voice through the air was a satanic trick. After all, the argument was that the devil was "the ruler of the kingdom of the air" (Eph. 2:2). We smile at that today, but those believers were right in this respect: Satan does travel through the air, creating havoc. In the Book of Job, God gave Satan the power to control lightning and a windstorm. But again I ask: does that mean that God has relegated such calamities to His hapless archrival?

Think about this: first, the God who permits natural disasters to happen could choose *not* to permit them to happen. In the very act of allowing them, He demonstrates that they fall within the boundaries of His providence and will. Notice that in the story of Job, Satan brought about the natural calamities of lightning and wind. But he could do this only when God signed off on it; he did it because God said, "Very well, then, everything he has is in your hands, but on the man himself do not lay a finger" (Job 1:12). Luther was right when he said, "Even the devil is God's devil."

Second, the Scriptures sometimes picture God as being in control of nature, even without secondary causes. When the disciples were at wit's end, expecting to drown, Christ awoke from His nap and said, "Quiet! Be still!" The effect was immediate: "Then the wind died down and it was completely calm" (Mark 4:39). The same Christ could have spoken similar words and the tidal wave in Honduras would have obeyed Him, and the rain that triggered the mud slides in Venezuela would not have turned into a flood.

Third, if the heavens declare the glory of God, if it is true that the Lord reveals His attributes through the positive side of nature, why would not the calamities of nature also reveal something about His other attributes? There is no hint in the Bible that the God who created the stars and keeps them in line is somehow removed from nature; if nature is to give us a balanced picture of God, we must see His judgment too. "The LORD does whatever pleases him, in the heavens and on the earth, in the seas and all their depths. He makes clouds rise from the ends of the earth; he sends lightning with the rain and brings out the wind from his storehouses" (Ps. 135:6–7).

Who sent the Flood during the time of Noah? God said, "I am going to bring floodwaters on the earth to destroy all life under the heavens, every creature that has the breath of life in it. Everything on earth will perish" (Gen. 6:17). God determined the timing, the duration, and the intensity of the rain. And it happened according to His word.

Who sent the plagues of Egypt, the hail and darkness that could be felt? Who caused the sun to "stand still" so that Joshua could win a war? Who sealed the heavens during the time of Elijah and then brought rain in response to his prayer? Who sent the earthquake when the sons of Korah rebelled against Moses? This event is of special interest: "As soon as he [Moses] finished saying all this, the ground under them split apart and the earth opened its mouth and swallowed them, with their households and all Korah's men and their possessions. They went down alive into the grave, with everything they owned; the earth closed over them, and they perished and were gone from the community" (Num. 16:31–33).

Can anyone doubt that God is the ultimate cause of these disasters?

The biblical writer leaves no doubt as to who caused the storm that forced the sailors to throw Jonah overboard: "Then the LORD sent a great wind on the sea, and such a violent storm arose that the ship threatened to break up." The sailors agonized about unloading their unwanted cargo, but we read, "They took Jonah and threw him overboard, and the raging sea grew calm" (Jon. 1:4, 15). Clearly, God was in charge.

What do all these stories have in common? First, we notice that God meticulously controlled these events. Whether an earthquake, a raging wind, or rainstorm, it came and left according to God's word. Second, these were, for the most part, acts of judgment; they were the means by which God expressed His hatred for disobedience. In Old Testament times these judgments generally separated the righteous from the wicked (this is not the case today, as we shall see in a moment). However, even back then we see that sometimes the righteous were victims of these judgments too. Job's children died not because they were wicked, but because God wanted to test their father.

If there is still some doubt in your mind that ultimately God has control of nature, let me ask: have you ever prayed for beautiful weather for a wedding? Have you ever prayed for rain at a time of drought? Have you ever prayed for protection during a lightning storm? Many people who do not believe that God controls the weather change their minds when a funnel cloud comes toward them.

The great nineteenth-century English preacher Charles Haddon Spurgeon was convinced that God's control of nature was exacting and complete:

> I believe that every particle of dust that dances in the sunbeam does not move an atom more or less than God wishes,—that every particle of spray that dashes against the steamboat has its orbit as well as the sun in the heavens,—that the chaff from the hand of the winnower is steered as the stars in their courses,—that the creeping of an aphid over a rosebud is as much fixed as the march of the devastating pestilence, and the fall of the sere leaves from the poplar is as fully ordained as the tumbling of an avalanche. He who believes in God must believe this truth.[4]

As might be expected, some people charged Spurgeon with fatalism, but he said that was a different doctrine altogether. "Fate says the thing is and must be; so it is decreed. But the true doctrine is—God has appointed this and that, not because it must be, but because it is best that it should be. *Fate is blind, but the destiny of the Scripture is full of eyes*" (emphasis mine).[5] God does nothing by chance but always acts for a purpose. Thus, while fate is stern and has no tears for sorrow, God's providences are kind and good; on this we can safely rest.

As I've mentioned, if you find a Christian who objects to the idea that God is ultimately in control of the weather, you will see him change his theology in a lightning storm. When he walks outside and feels the sizzle of electricity in the air, he will pray for safety. We can try to distance God from these events, but the moment we bow our heads to pray, we know that He is in charge. The ministers in San Francisco were right in giving God thanks that the earthquake came early in the morning when there was little traffic on the expressways. They were wrong, however, for saying that God was not responsible for the tragedy. Of course He was. Both biblically and logically, it can be no other way.

Of course, I am not entirely happy with the word *responsibility* when we apply it to God; for us responsibility usually means accountability. God is accountable to no one. "Our God is in heaven; he does whatever pleases him" (Ps. 115:3).

## WHEN WE FIGHT NATURE, ARE WE FIGHTING GOD?

In fighting against natural disasters, do we fight against God? In his book *The Plague,* French writer Albert Camus wrestles with the question of whether battling the plague means that we are battling God. In the story, rats bring a plague to the city of Oran at the beginning of World War II. The choice, says Camus, is either we join the doctor and fight against God or we join the passive priest and be antihumanitarian.[6] If God stands behind nature, if calamities come according to His will and purpose, in fighting nature are we not fighting God?

The answer is *no.* We can fight the plague (or any other disaster) and not fight God. Whatever control God exercises over nature, the Bible is clear that *nature is not God.* Christianity stands in sharp opposition to pantheism, which teaches that "all is God and God is all." In fact, *nature is given to us so that we might subdue it.* In the original mandate to Adam, God commanded him to "fill the earth and subdue it. Rule over the fish of the sea and the birds of the air and over every living creature that moves on the ground" (Gen. 1:28). And after the Fall, man would strive against nature, fighting against thorns and thistles. He would earn a living by painful toil and the sweat of his brow.

As I explained, God usually exercises His control of nature through secondary causes; He might use the devil as in the case of Job, or use the natural laws already in place. He uses the weather patterns for tornadoes, the faults beneath the earth for earthquakes. God uses these immediate causes to accomplish His direction and control of nature, but He invites us to oppose such calamities.

The Westminster Confession of Faith takes note of this important distinction, and though worded in formal language, I encourage you to read these lines carefully: "Although, in relation to the foreknowledge and decree of God, the first cause, all things come to pass immutably and infallibly; yet, by the same providence, he ordereth them to fall out according to the nature of second causes, either necessarily, freely or contingently."⁷ We should control nature to the best of our ability. God uses nature to both bless and challenge us, to feed and instruct us. God intends these forces, like the devil, for our eternal benefit that we might, as far as possible, overcome them. Yes, we can and *must* fight the plague.

In fact, believers should be willing to help those who are in distress even at great personal risk. Luther, when confronted with the question of whether Christians should help the sick and dying when the plague came to Wittenberg, said, "This is God's decree and punishment to which we must patiently submit and serve our neighbor, risking our lives in this manner as St. John teaches, 'If Christ laid down his life for us, we ought to lay down our lives for the brethren' (I John 3:16)."⁸

Luther also wrote:

If it be God's will that evil come upon us and destroy us, none of our precautions will help us. Everybody must take this to heart: first of all, if he feels bound to remain where death rages in order to serve his neighbor, let him commend himself to God and say, "Lord, I am in thy hands; thou hast kept me here; thy will be done. I am thy lowly creature. Thou canst kill me or preserve me in the pestilence in the same way as if I were in fire, water, drought or any other danger."⁹

Yes, the plague was "God's decree," but yes, we must do what we can to save the lives of the sick and minister to the dying. We should thank God when Christians take the opportunity to rescue the wounded when a disaster strikes. And if one dies while helping others, as Luther said, let the will of God be done.

See Jesus weep at the tomb of Lazarus, and hear His groans: "Jesus, once more deeply moved, came to the tomb. It was a cave with a stone laid across the entrance." After the stone was removed, Jesus shouted, "Lazarus, come out!" and the dead man came to life in the presence of the startled onlookers (John 11:38, 43). The Jesus who allowed Lazarus to die is the same Jesus who raised him from the dead. Just so, the God who created the laws of nature that "take their course" is the same God who invites us to fight against these natural forces. We can try to stave off death as long as possible through medicine and technology, but eventually we will be overcome by its power. Yet in the end we win, for Christ came to conquer the decay of fallen nature.

But if God is the ultimate cause of all things, dare we charge Him with evil? Are not all His gifts good, perfect, and helpful? We continue our reflections.


## DARE WE CHARGE GOD WITH EVIL?

In the Book of Job, the young theologian Elihu says of God:

> He says to the snow, "Fall on the earth,"
>     and to the rain shower, "Be a mighty downpour."
> . . . The breath of God produces ice,
>     and the broad waters become frozen.
> He loads the clouds with moisture;
>     he scatters his lightning through them.
> At his direction they swirl around
>     over the face of the whole earth
>     to do whatever he commands them.
> He brings the clouds to punish men,
>     or to water his earth and show his love.
>
> (Job 37:6, 10–13)

"He brings the clouds to punish men, or to water his earth and show his love." We like to think that God is in control of only the positive side of nature: the sunshine, the irresistible lure of calm waters, and the starry heavens. But as we have learned, God is in charge of the totality of nature. If the goodness of God is evident in the blessings of nature, His judgments are evident in the "cursing" of nature. Either way, nature exists to instruct us, to help us understand God better.

The starry heavens reflect the glory of God; calm winds and sunshine remind us of the mercy of God; the upheavals of nature demonstrate the judgment of God. If the former anticipates the beauty of heaven, the latter anticipates the suffering of hell. "Consider therefore the kindness and sternness of God: sternness to those who fell, but kindness to you, provided that you continue in his kindness" (Rom. 11:22). We should not be surprised that nature is both kind and stern.

We complain about natural disasters, but we often are silent about the rain and sunshine that God sends without partiality to the righteous and unrighteous. In fact, the reason we should be kind to our enemies is because of this promise: "But love your enemies, do good to them, and lend to them without expecting to get anything back. Then your reward will be great, and you will be sons of the Most High, because he is kind to the ungrateful and wicked" (Luke 6:35). How unthankful we are for the times when the earth does not shake, when the tornadoes do not blow, and when the floods do not come. "Because of the LORD's great love we are not consumed, for his compassions never fail. They are new every morning; great is your faithfulness" (Lam. 3:22–23).

How can God be good when He permits (or does) things that seem so destructive and hurtful to human beings? Surely if we had the power to prevent an earthquake, if we could have stopped that tidal wave in Honduras, we would have done so. Just think of the children who are made orphans when a natural disaster strikes, the new widows and widowers, the depleted resources, and the fresh graves. Should we charge God with evil?

First, let us candidly agree that God plays by a different set of rules.

If you were standing beside a swimming pool and watched a toddler fall in and did not pull the child out, your negligence would be cause for prosecution. Yet God watches children drown or, for that matter, starve every day and does not intervene. He sends drought, creating scarcity of food; He sends tidal waves, wiping out homes and crops.

We are obligated to keep people alive as long as possible; if God were held to that standard, no one would ever die. He could keep the whole population of the world alive indefinitely. What for us would be criminal, is for God an everyday occurrence.

Why the difference? He is the Creator; we are the creatures. Because He is the giver of life, He also has the right to take life. He has a long-term agenda that is much more complex than keeping people alive as long as possible. Death and destruction are a part of His plan. "'For my thoughts are not your thoughts, neither are your ways my ways,' declares the LORD. 'As the heavens are higher than the earth, so are my ways higher than your ways and my thoughts than your thoughts'" (Isa. 55:8–9).

Did you ever realize that not all of the Ten Commandments apply to God? For example, He cannot steal, for He owns everything. He does not bear false witness, but having neither father or mother, He must of necessity honor only Himself. God does not often strike a person dead, but through disease, disaster, and various other calamities He does take human life regularly, daily, hourly.

The famous philosopher John Stuart Mill wrote that natural disasters prove that God is neither good nor omnipotent, for if He were, He would meticulously dispense suffering and happiness to the world, with each getting exactly what he/she deserved. Given the randomness of natural disasters, Mill writes, "Not even on the most distorted and contracted theory of good which ever was framed by religious or philosophical fanaticism can the government of nature be made to resemble the work of a being once both good and omnipotent."[10]

Mill forgets, however, a second principle, that final rewards and punishments are not meted out in this life; indeed, the Scriptures teach that the righteous often endure the most fearful calamities. In fact, God is both good and omnipotent, but He always acts from the standpoint of eternity rather than time; He makes all decisions with an infinite perspective. If you were to think of a measuring tape that goes to the farthest star, the existence of planet earth would only be a hairline. Thus, what we view from the standpoint of time, God sees in a vast panorama of eternity. There will be plenty of time for punishment and reward. We believe that God had a good and all-wise purpose for the heartrending tragedy in Turkey that took thousands of lives. Indeed, author John Piper contends that "he had hundreds of thousands of purposes, most of which will remain hidden to us until we are able to grasp them at the end of the age."[11]

Third, God does not delight in the suffering of humanity. Surely this would be inconsistent with His basic nature of loving the world. But God does take delight in executing His judgments. Moses told the Israelites the consequences if they sinned: "Just as it pleased the LORD to make you prosper and increase in number, so it will please him to ruin and destroy you. You will be uprooted from the land you are entering to possess" (Deut. 28:63). The reason is obvious: He delights in defending His glory; He is jealous that this happen.

Finally, as finite beings, we cannot judge an infinite being. God is not obligated to tell us all that He is up to. It is not necessary for us to see God's eternal purposes in order for us to believe that He has such a plan and that He knows what He is doing. As Paul reminded an imaginary objector to God's sovereignty, the clay has no right to judge the potter. It is not necessary for us to know God's purposes before we bow before His authority. And the fact that we trust God though He has not revealed the details to us is something that delights His heart. "Without faith it is impossible to please God" (Heb. 11:6).

William Cowper put the mysteries of God in perspective:

> God moves in a mysterious way
> His wonders to perform
> He plants His footsteps in the sea,

And rides upon the storm
Deep in unfathomable mines
Of never-failing skill
He treasures up His bright designs,
And works His sovereign will
Ye fearful saints, fresh courage take;
The clouds ye so much dread
Are big with mercy, and shall break
In blessing on your head
Judge not the Lord by feeble sense,
But trust Him for His grace
Behind a frowning providence
He hides a smiling face
His purposes will ripen fast,
Unfolding every hour;
The bud may have a bitter taste,
But sweet will be the flow'r
Blind unbelief is sure to err,
And scan His work in vain;
God is His own interpreter
And He will make it plain.[12]

"Grieve not because thou understandest not life's mystery," wrote a wise man, "behind the veil is concealed many a delight."[13] The trusting believer knows this is so.

## WHAT IS THE MESSAGE
## OF NATURAL DISASTERS?

When Jesus was told how Pilate had butchered a group of Galileans and their blood mixed with pagan sacrifices, He answered, "Do you think that these Galileans were worse sinners than all the other Galileans because they suffered this way? I tell you, no! But unless you repent, you too will all perish" (Luke 13:2–3). Of course His answer does not surprise us, since martyrdom is often a credit to one's faith; indeed, Jesus Himself was brutally murdered.

But then He continues: "Or those eighteen who died when the tower in Siloam fell on them—do you think they were more guilty than all the others living in Jerusalem? I tell you, no! But unless you repent, you too will all perish" (Luke 13:4–5). Disasters are a picture of judgment, but those who die in them are not greater sinners than others who are spared such a fate.

This is an important distinction between the Old Testament and the New. In former times, God ruled the Jewish nation directly and dealt with them as a group. Thus there was an immediate cause/effect relationship between their obedience and the cooperation of natural forces. God tied His blessing of the people directly to the cooperation of nature. "When I shut up the heavens so that there is no rain, or command locusts to devour the land or send a plague among my people, if my people, who are called by my name, will humble themselves and pray and seek my face and turn from their wicked ways, then will I hear from heaven and will forgive their sin and will heal their land" (2 Chron. 7:13–14). In the New Testament era, God gives good crops sometimes even when a nation turns from God, as we can see in the United States today. Just as the evil are blessed with the righteous, so the righteous often die with the wicked in the natural disasters that come our way.

We cannot pretend to understand all that God has in mind when tragedies come to a country or, for that matter, to a single family or person. But natural disasters are God's megaphone, shouting to us messages that we should be quick to learn.

First, death is inevitable. When you read the obituaries of those who have died in sudden calamities, you should visualize your own name in the column. All of us know someone who has been unexpectedly killed. At such moments death is so real to us that we remember that we, too, could die without warning. Natural disasters are a reminder of our mortality.

I read about one couple who left California for fear of earthquakes and died in a tornado in Missouri. Life is a loan from God. He gives it and He takes it, whenever and however He wills. This sounds heartless, but C. S. Lewis was right when he pointed out that natural disasters do not increase death; all the victims of these disasters would have to die by virtue of old age. Cruel as it sounds, the fact is that death is certain for all of us, whether by cancer, an accident, or a natural disaster. We'll all die from something, for the Bible teaches that death is a scheduled, divine appointment.

Second, natural disasters remind us that judgment is coming. "Unless you repent, you will all likewise perish" (Luke 13:3, NASB). Obviously, the unrepentant will not necessarily die in a similar calamity, but they will be carried away in judgment without warning.

Jesus predicted that end-time calamities were a sign of the end of the age. "There will be famines and earthquakes in various places. All these are the beginning of birth pains" (Matt. 24:7–8). The convulsions of nature will be a part of God's sovereign judgment. Here is a future "natural disaster":

> I watched as he opened the sixth seal. There was a great earthquake.
> The sun turned black like sackcloth made of goat hair, the whole
> moon turned blood red, and the stars in the sky fell to earth, as late
> figs drop from a fig tree when shaken by a strong wind. The sky
> receded like a scroll, rolling up, and every mountain and island was
> removed from its place.
>
> Then the kings of the earth, the princes, the generals, the rich, the
> mighty, and every slave and every free man hid in caves and among
> the rocks of the mountains. They called to the mountains and the
> rocks, "Fall on us and hide us from the face of him who sits on the
> throne and from the wrath of the Lamb! For the great day of their
> wrath has come, and who can stand?"
>
> (Rev. 6:12–17)

Many people say that they cannot believe that God would judge people severely; hell, especially, they consider unthinkable. But if He allowed six million Jews, among them hundreds of thousands of children, to be mercilessly massacred, then perhaps it is not too difficult to believe in the terrors of a final judgment and hell. The God of liberal theology, the God who seeks the happiness of His creation to the best of His ability, the God who would never judge us for our sins or commit sinners to hell—such a God does not exist in the Bible and is contradicted by the natural disasters in the world. He does not delight in human suffering, but He does delight in the triumph of truth and justice and the completion of His hidden purposes.

The final lesson is that we escape coming judgment by repentance. Recall that when the *Titanic* sank, it went under with 1,522 people knowingly going to a watery grave. Even if we attribute the sinking to a series of human errors, God most assuredly was able to keep it from sinking without any violation of the human will. This is another reminder that the God who permits such unthinkable tragedies is one to fear.

After the news of the *Titanic* tragedy reached the world, the challenge was how to inform the relatives whether their loved ones were among the dead or the living. At the White Star office in Liverpool, England, a huge sign was set up; one side read, "Known to Be Saved," and the other, "Known to Be Lost." Hundreds of people gathered to watch the signs. When a messenger brought new information, the question was: To which side would he go? And whose name would he write on the cardboard?[14]

Although the travelers on the *Titanic* were designated either first, second, or third class, after the ship went down there were only two categories: the saved and the lost. Just so, we can divide people into many different classes based on geography, race, education, and wealth. But in the day of judgment, there will be only two classes: the saved and the lost.

Perhaps in heaven a mother will be looking for her son, wondering if he will arrive safely behind the pearly gates. Wives will wait for husbands, and parents for children.

Today God shouts from heaven, "Except you repent, you will perish!"

## A PERSONAL RESPONSE

In the face of the terrifying upheavals of nature, our first response should be worship. When Job lost his ten children to a windstorm, he did not know the prologue to his book; he did not know that Satan and God had had a dialogue and that he had been singled out for a special trial. Without explanation, without Job's knowing the fine print of God's purposes, a natural disaster wiped out his children. With ten fresh graves on the side of a hill, he faced a choice, and he chose worship: "Naked I came from my mother's womb, and naked I will depart. The LORD gave and the LORD has taken away; may the name of the LORD be praised" (Job 1:20).

The next day, things went from bad to worse. By then Satan had permission from God to smite Job with "painful sores from the soles of his feet to the top of his head" (Job 2:7). Again, Job had to choose what to do: should he worship or curse?

Satan told God that if Job had his possessions taken from him, he would curse God to his face (Job 1:11). While Satan predicted that Job would curse God, and though Job's wife, unable to bear his suffering, encouraged it with the cryptic remark, "Curse God and die!" Job would have no part of it. With the keen insight of a theologian, he corrected her. "Shall we accept good from God, and not trouble?" (Job 2:9–10). He knew that both the good times and trouble came from God. He would bless and not curse.

Can we trust a God who controls nature? Yes, for unless He does, we would be subject to the whims of impersonal fate. I find no consolation in accepting the premise that God is not the ultimate cause of natural disasters. If the devil creates tornadoes and hurricanes without God's approval, I could die in a disaster before my appointed time. Perhaps God still has work for me to do, but a stray bolt of lightning over which

God has chosen to have no control might strike me as I walk along the sidewalk. But if the weather is His to route, then I rest with the confidence that my life is ordered according to His will and plan. *If nature is out of God's hands, then my life is also out of His hands.*

Far from discouraging faith, God's control of nature encourages it! If God is sovereign, then we can have the confidence that "all things work together for good" (Rom. 8:28, KJV). We do not believe in fate, but in a specific purpose ordained by an all-wise God. Natural disasters might drive some people away from God; for others they have the opposite effect—they drive us toward Him, because they remind us of what is temporary and what is permanent.

When the earth shakes under your feet, or when a tornado crosses your street, you take cover, but ultimately we must flee into the arms of the only One who is able to shelter us. No matter how many things move in this world, we can always find *terra firma*, solid ground, in the consolations of the Almighty. We are reminded that all things pass away and only what is eternal abides.

The righteous sons of Korah (the psalm-writers, not the earthquake victims) knew that when all gives way, God abides. They invite us to recognize God's majesty and run to Him for safety.

> God is our refuge and strength,
>     an ever-present help in trouble.
> Therefore we will not fear, though the earth give way
>     and the mountains fall into the heart of the sea,
> though its waters roar and foam
>     and the mountains quake with their surging.
> There is a river whose streams make glad the city of God,
>     the holy place where the Most High dwells.
> God is within her, she will not fall;
>     God will help her at break of day.
> Nations are in uproar, kingdoms fall;
>     he lifts his voice, the earth melts.

The LORD Almighty is with us;
>    the God of Jacob is our fortress.
Come and see the works of the LORD,
>    the desolations he has brought on the earth.
He makes wars cease to the ends of the earth;
>    he breaks the bow and shatters the spear,
>    he burns the shields with fire.
"Be still, and know that I am God;
>    I will be exalted among the nations,
>    I will be exalted in the earth."
The LORD Almighty is with us;
>    the God of Jacob is our fortress.

(Ps. 46)

**LIE 7**

# God Does Not Know Our Decisions Before We Make Them

LET US TAKE AN IMAGINARY JOURNEY. Suppose someone has been at your side every day of your life, recording everything you ever did. He includes the number of times you blinked your eyes, took a step, sat down, stood up, or combed your hair.

Let us also suppose that every word you have spoken is part of his record. He transcribes each utterance: the good, the bad, the ugly, your whispered words as well as your public ones. Imagine the storehouse: it is said that the average person speaks enough words in a lifetime to fill a library of books!

Let us also suppose that your companion records your thoughts—that stream of consciousness that winds its way through your mind every waking moment. All of your contemplations—good, indifferent, and sinful—he is accurately listing. Picture this: if he adds these thoughts to your actions and words, he will have many more libraries of information, all about you!

Now let us take this a step further: let us suppose that this library included not only information that was true of you, but also information that would have been true of you *if* you had been born into a different family, a different culture, and a different country. In fact, let us suppose the library was so exhaustive that it included everything that would have been true of you in every conceivable circumstance: what you would have done, said, or thought in every family of the world, every century, every year.

Question: Did God have all of this knowledge in His possession a thousand years ago or, for that matter, from all eternity? Or does He have to wait until we arrive on planet earth to know what we are going to decide to do, think, and say?

We touched on this in a previous chapter, but I want to expand on it here because it is both timely and unspeakably important. Today evangelical theologians are debating the question of whether God has exhaustive knowledge. Some insist that His knowledge is limited: He knows much more than we do, but He does not know our decisions until we make them. After all, the argument goes, we are free creatures— so free that not even God knows the actions we will take or the thoughts we will think until we actually do and think them.

As for the future, they say, God knows only potentialities, not actualities. When we face a decision, He knows what our options are, He knows what we are likely to choose, but He finds out what our choice is only when we make it. Of course in the end God wins because no surprise stymies His power or plans, just like a superior chess player who eventually will checkmate an amateur. But He does not know what his opponents' moves will be until they make them.

Should you be interested in this debate, or is it purely academic? I think you should be very concerned, because this view of what is called the "openness of God" could undermine everything that the Christian church has held to be important. If a missile left a launch pad one degree off its proper trajectory, it would be hundreds of miles off the mark when it reached the vicinity of its target. What appears to be a minor error in theology becomes critical once we understand its implications. Just so, the belief that God is finite in knowledge might appear to be an acceptable deviation from historic Christianity, but in the end it destroys our faith in God.

Stay with me and I'll explain.

## THE ORIGIN OF THE IDEA OF A FINITE GOD

Is this notion that God's knowledge is limited a new insight? No, during the time of the Reformation a man named Faustus Socinus (1539–1604) accepted only those parts of the Bible that seemed reasonable to him. One of his and his followers' goals was to revive the Greek concept of man's absolute free will; some of these ancient philosophers argued that to be completely free, one must be free of any control of the gods, even free of their knowledge. In fact, it is said that when spiders spun webs across the eyelids of the Greek images (their gods), the people more regularly visited their temple of worship! The less the gods knew about them, the more comfortable they felt.

The Socinians who accepted these Greek ideas did not want to outrightly deny God's omniscience, so they just redefined the term. Omniscience, they said, meant that God knows only what is knowable, and the decisions of free creatures are unknowable. So, since God can't know the unknowable, He does not know our decisions until we make them.

William James (1842–1910) is perhaps one of the most famous defenders of this idea. He affirmed that man was radically free and that God was finite, trying His best to eradicate evil in the world, but failing. God, said James, does not know the future: "He cannot foresee exactly what any one actual move of his adversary may be. He knows, however, the possible moves of the latter; and he knows in advance how to meet each of them by a move of his own which leads in the direction of victory." God's knowledge, he says, "is just like ours."[1] Basing his ideas on his own rational thoughts rather than the Bible, he even posited the idea that there might be many gods in the universe, not just one.

We should not be surprised that such theories flourish among theological liberals; after all, if the Bible is not authoritative, man is free to create whatever God suits his fancy. What is surprising is that some theologians who want to be thought of as evangelicals hold some of James's views and teach them to young men and women who are training for the ministry. This heresy is not just in the world; it is in the believing church.

Perhaps Clark Pinnock, the professor of theology at McMaster

Divinity College in Ontario whom I introduced previously, is the person best known in contemporary circles for perpetuating this idea of a finite God. Many years ago, I studied under Dr. Pinnock and found him to be a kind and engaging man with an active mind. At that time he was beginning to rethink his theological heritage and denied such doctrines as the inerrancy of the Bible and the complete omniscience of God. Pinnock writes: "God . . . interacts with his creatures in a changing situation. His experience of the world is open and not closed. He learns about our decisions as they happen, not before they happen. . . . His experience of the world is open and he is involved in the ongoing course of events."[2]

At least a few other theologians have followed his lead. For example, Dr. Greg Boyd, at the time of this writing a professor at Bethel College, writes:

> In the Christian view, God knows all of reality—everything there is to know. But to assume He knows ahead of time how every person is going to freely act assumes that each person's free activity is already there to know—even before he freely does it! But it's not. If we have been given freedom, we create the reality of our own decisions by making them. And until we make them, they don't exist. Thus, in my view, at least, there simply isn't anything to know until we make it there to know. So God can't foreknow the good or bad decisions of the people He creates until He creates these people and they, in turn, create their decisions.[3]

Dr. Boyd, like William James, reduces the future to what is "knowable," and the free actions of men lie outside of that perimeter.

Richard Rice of the Seventh-Day Adventists further argues that the future is so "open" that God could not know in advance whether Christ would sin when the devil tempted Him. Yes, the future is so open that just possibly Christ could have failed in His mission, and God could not have foreseen that His plan was in ruins.[4]

Why would these theologians want to limit God's knowledge?

First, they think this limitation is necessary to preserve human freedom. As Pinnock writes, "If God is changeless in every aspect of his being and knows history, there cannot be genuine freedom."[5] Let's follow what he is saying: all of us agree that if God knows our decisions ahead of time, then we will make the choices God knows we will make. Thus if God knows the future in detail, the future is in some sense "fixed."

Think of it this way: foreknowledge implies inevitability. If God knew that Cain would kill Abel, it could *not* "not happen." If God was ignorant of this impending murder, Cain was more free and unlimited in his options. If God knows the future, He knows who will be saved and who will be lost; this infallible knowledge means that the future will turn out as God sees it. So these theologians want to deny that God knows these things to keep the future "open."

Second, these writers wish to protect God from the charge of ordaining evil. If God didn't know that Lucifer was going to sin, it appears that God is less responsible than if He knew it ahead of time. If God knew that some of His angels would rebel, He could have used His power to create a different future. But, the argument goes, He didn't know about their choice to disobey until it happened, so He had to adjust to it. In a word, the more ignorant God is of what is going to happen, the less responsibility He has for the outcome.

God's role in this scenario is that of an interested observer of the happenings in His world. He chooses to intervene as little as possible in the affairs of men, giving us plenty of room for free will. Though He does not know what our next step will be, He hopes for the best and adjusts to the worst. God triumphs by being able to cope with whatever happens in the world.

Proponents of this "open view" of God cite several texts as evidence. For example, they suggest that the Scripture states that God "repented" of several of His own actions (Gen. 6:6; 1 Sam. 15:11; 2 Sam. 24:16, KJV). The argument these theologians make is this: how could God have regretted something He created if He was sure what would happen before He created it? The implication is that God could not regret something He foreknew.

But as we shall see in a moment, it is obvious that God foresaw the devastation sin would cause, and that He would endure pain because of it. "Yet," as John Piper points out, "he does not regard his choices as mistakes that he would do differently if only he foreknew what was coming."[6] In other words, as we saw in chapter 4, God chose to suffer when Christ died; He chose to be grieved because of men's actions. This in no way means that He was ignorant of the sorrow He would have because of His creatures' rebellion.

The "open" view of God deviates from mainstream Christian theology, which has always taught that God knows our decisions before we make them. Arminians (who emphasize free will) and Calvinists (who stress God's sovereignty in our choices) have had their differences, but they have always agreed that God knows the future exhaustively; He knows everything, including our future decisions.

So in this chapter, I am not considering the Arminian/Calvinistic debate, rather this "open view of God" which is a departure from evangelical theology. I ask the question again: is this development a serious or minor doctrinal difference? Before we answer, let us spell out the consequences of this view of God.

## SOME DIFFICULTIES OF BELIEVING IN A FINITE GOD

If one string of a violin is out of tune, you must either adjust it so that it will be in harmony with the other strings, or you must adjust the other strings to be in harmony with the errant string. Just so, I hope to show that once God's knowledge is compromised, everything—but especially our confidence in Him—is jeopardized. In the end we shall see that God's exhaustive knowledge terrifies us, but thankfully, it is also a pillow on which we can rest our weary souls. Let me give some difficulties with this "open" view of God.

## The Statements of Scripture

The notion that God does not foreknow the decisions of His creatures is contrary to explicit statements of Scripture. The God of Isaiah knew the future exhaustively.

> Remember the former things long past,
> For I am God, and there is no other;
> I am God, and there is no one like Me,
> Declaring the end from the beginning
> And from ancient times things which have not been done,
> Saying, "My purpose will be established,
> And I will accomplish all My good pleasure."
>
> (Isa. 46:9–10, NASB)

How could God possibly make known the end from the beginning if He did not know that Lucifer would rebel and Adam and Eve would sin? And how can He know exactly how everything will end if He does not know the subsequent choices we and millions of others would make? If He were ignorant of these matters, He would have little to declare.

Yes, of course, those who believe in a limited God argue that He knows how it will all end, because He can exercise power (never infringing on free will, to be sure), like a chess player who wins in the end. But the matter is more serious than that. According to the open view of God, He cannot be absolutely certain that we will not have a nuclear holocaust tomorrow. Some deranged individuals might make a reckless decision to blow up the planet; God does not stop them, for they have free will and He has chosen to let evil run its course. Suddenly, though, if some governmental power ignites a nuclear war, God faces the reality of responding to the end of the world before He thought it would probably take place.

David would not have accepted the notion of a limited God. He wrote, "Great is our Lord and mighty in power; his understanding has no limit" (Ps. 147:5). Interestingly, God Himself makes His foreknowledge the test of His superiority over idols. He taunts idols, ridiculing them because they do not know the future.

> "Present your case," says the LORD.
> "Set forth your arguments," says Jacob's King.
> "Bring in your idols to tell us
> what is going to happen.
> Tell us what the former things were,
> so that we may consider them
> and know their final outcome.
> Or declare to us the things to come,
> tell us what the future holds,
> so we may know that you are gods.
> Do something, whether good or bad,
> so that we will be dismayed and filled with fear."
>
> (Isa. 41:21–23)

"Tell us what the future holds, so we may know that you are gods!" Do the idols take up His challenge? Of course not. God mocks them, "But you are less than nothing and your works are utterly worthless; he who chooses you is detestable." A few verses later He concludes, "See, they are all false! Their deeds amount to nothing; their images are but wind and confusion" (Isa. 41:24, 29). One distinguishing characteristic between a false god and the Almighty is that God knows the future infallibly.

## The Accuracy of Prophecy

If God does not know what decisions people will eventually make, hundreds of prophecies in the Bible just might not have come to pass. For example, how could Jesus know that Judas would betray Him? This calls for a more detailed analysis.

Picture the scene: after Judas betrayed Jesus, Peter drew his sword in what appeared to be an act of bravery, and Jesus responded, "Put your sword back in its place. . . . Do you think I cannot call on my Father, and he will at once put at my disposal more than twelve legions of angels? But how then would the Scriptures be fulfilled that say it must happen in this way?" (Matt. 26:52–54). In context Christ could have meant only one thing: the betrayal, the arrest, and His impending death *must* happen in the way they were unfolding.

According to Pinnock, God did not know that Judas would betray Jesus until he did so; there might have been some hints along the way, some circumstances that pointed in that direction, but Judas or the priests could have had a change of heart. And if Judas might have had a change of heart so might the Jews during Jesus' mock trials, and the Romans, too, might have backed out of the ghastly deed. So it follows that not even God was sure that Jesus would actually be crucified. All the key players might have decided that Jesus was not worth the trouble. Just let Him live.

That, of course, is not the teaching of Scripture. Centuries earlier, God knew that Judas's parents would marry at a certain time, that they would have a male child who would grow up in a region through which Jesus would pass when He walked this earth. But God would also have to know Judas's grandparents, when they would marry, what children they would have, and so on, ad infinitum. And there was no possibility that Judas would die in infancy; nor could Judas have fallen sick that afternoon, unable to betray Jesus, for God knew from all eternity that it *must* happen in that way.

Pinnock suggests that if Plan A fails, God has Plan B. Maybe someone else would have crucified Christ if the key players had backed out. But if Plan A failed, what makes us think that Plan B would have been successful? Nor could God be certain about Plans C and D. Imagine Jesus coming to earth, all the prophecies notwithstanding, and no one puts Him to death!

A bit of sober reflection makes us realize that this is not what the

Bible teaches; the death of Christ was a certain event from before the foundation of the world. As Peter and John declared to God in prayer, "Indeed Herod and Pontius Pilate met together with the Gentiles and the people of Israel in this city to conspire against your holy servant Jesus, whom you anointed. They did what your power and will had decided beforehand should happen" (Acts 4:27–28). Peter said essentially the same thing in an earlier message: "This man was handed over to you by God's set purpose and foreknowledge; and you, with the help of wicked men, put him to death by nailing him to the cross" (Acts 2:23). Christ died as God *determined* beforehand; it happened according to God's set purpose.

Jesus knew infallibly that Peter would betray Him three times. "I tell you, Peter, before the rooster crows today, you will deny three times that you know me" (Luke 22:34). The absolute knowledge that Peter would sin, how often he would sin, and when he would sin, was known to Jesus. And Jesus gave the reason for His prediction in John 13:19: "I am telling you before it comes to pass, so that when it does occur, you may believe that I am He" (NASB). As John Piper notes, "His foreknowledge of 'all the things that were coming upon him' was an essential aspect of his glory as the incarnate Word, the Son of God. The denial of this foreknowledge is, I believe John would say, (whether intended or not) an assault on the deity of Christ."[7]

Of dozens of other prophecies that prove that God knows the future decisions of men, I shall give only one more. One hundred and fifty years before Cyrus was born, God named him, predicted that he would be the king of Persia, and foreknew one of his most important foreign policy decisions (Isa. 44:24–28; 45:1–6). Again, think of all that God had to know in order to make that prediction: He had to know every one of Cyrus's ancestors, whom each would marry, and the various members in the family chain; each would have to live so that Cyrus would be born. God also had to know who the players would be in the power struggle over the kingship of Persia and that Cyrus would win. Then God had to know that the Jews would be in the land of Persia by that time and that Cyrus would give a decree that they return to their land. It is unthinkable that God could have such knowledge without knowing the future decisions of men.

## The Omnipotence of God

The "open view" of God erodes our confidence in the omnipotence of God. This matter will become clearer in the next chapter, but for now I simply raise this issue: there is a link between the foreknowledge of God and the omnipotence of God. To put it more directly, God knows the future because He is involved in planning it. And if He is not involved in planning it, as the "open view" asserts, then the events of this world are not being directed to an appointed end. God has surrendered His power and quite literally things are presently out of control, even though God will somehow work out His plan in the end.

If this sounds like an overstatement of the "open view," listen to the words of Greg Boyd, who writes that his view "presupposes the reality of radical contingency and of genuine risk. It further presupposes that this risk has sometimes gone bad, even on a cosmic scale, and that this has turned the earth into a veritable war zone."[8] The question we would have to ask is, if God is omnipotent, why would things have "gone bad" for Him? Of course I do not dispute that things in this world have soured, but I want to assert that it is not because God took a risk that backfired. I will cover more of this in the next chapter.

## The Trustworthiness of God

Finally, the "open view" of God undermines our trust in Him. A drunk is cruising along the highway at seventy miles per hour, and God has no more knowledge of what that driver will do than the pilot of the chopper overhead. The Almighty cannot foresee whether there will be an accident or whether the driver will make it safely home. (After all, no one's free will is as unpredictable as that of a drunk cruising along the highway.) Meanwhile you are driving the opposite direction, and the driver turns into your car. You are killed instantly.

Not only was the decision of the drunk unknown to God, so was your death. You arrive in heaven that evening. And although God knew this *could* have happened, He did not know that it *would*. So God does not know who will live or die today; He does not know who will be saved today or in the future; He does not know how or when Antichrist will actually arise. He must, in effect, read the daily newspaper along with us to keep up to date on His world.

Can you trust a God like that? Can you trust a God who does not know in the morning that you will be dead that evening? Does not the "open view" of God make us feel sorry for Him, since He can only react as best He can to the unforeseen decisions of Satan and men? Personally, I am grateful that the "open view" does not represent the God of the Bible.

Why do I feel so deeply about these matters? Because I want to commend to you a God in whom you can safely trust. A God who was not caught off guard when Lucifer sinned; a God who was not surprised when Adam and Eve chose to disobey; a God who knew that Cain would kill Abel. A God who knows exactly what you will encounter next week and next year; a God who can keep you alive until your work on earth is done.

Greg Boyd writes, "Just as salvation through faith alone was rediscovered by Luther, the feature that God is open has been recovered."[9] But this is one view best left in the past with the Socinians and William James, who did so much to destroy the faith of many. The notion that God does not have exhaustive knowledge is a defective view of the Almighty. Superficially, it might appear as if it fits within the framework of evangelical theology, but taken to its logical conclusions, it not only is a defective view but a heretical view of God as well.

## GOD'S PERSONAL KNOWLEDGE OF US

Psalm 139 teaches us about the exhaustive knowledge of God. And although David is primarily emphasizing the Father's present knowledge of us, he does speak of God's foreknowledge. I'm sure David would be scandalized at the suggestion that there is something in our future that is unknown to the Almighty.

## God Knows Us Entirely

"O LORD, you have searched me and you know me," he begins. "You know when I sit and when I rise; you perceive my thoughts from afar. You discern my going out and my lying down; you are familiar with all my ways" (Ps. 139:1–3). Can you reflect on how many times you sat down and stood up yesterday? I can't. Yet God was there the whole time. Can I remember the general content of my thoughts yesterday? Not very well, and most assuredly not accurately. Yet God knows all these things with impeccable exactness. And He does not know yesterday better than He knows twenty years ago. All these things are present to Him.

David now turns from his actions and thoughts to his words: "Before a word is on my tongue you know it completely, O LORD" (v. 4). Even if I do not know what I am going to say, even if I have no idea what I will be thinking or saying next Thursday afternoon, God does. My unformed thoughts and words are like seeds, and their fruit is known in advance to the keeper of the heart. My future thoughts and deeds are fully known.

"You hem me in—behind and before; you have laid your hand upon me" (v. 5). David meditates on the fact that he is continually encircled within God's knowledge. He may sleep and forget God, but the Almighty never sleeps. David says, in effect, "Your gaze is constantly upon me." A prisoner told what it was like to be constantly watched by a guard, day and night. No matter when he looked up, a pair of eyes stared at him through the bars. We feel uneasy when a man watches us because we don't know his intent, but when God sees us, we can be either terrified or comforted.

If you have ever been misunderstood, misrepresented, or otherwise taken advantage of, you will be reassured to know that God knows.

Perhaps we are pushed into a corner, believing that we have no one in this world we can trust, no one who really understands us and our story. We can take comfort in the assurance that God has all the facts.

No wonder David continues, "Such knowledge is too wonderful for me, too lofty for me to attain" (v. 6). We can't get our minds around the vast information that is ever present to the Almighty. We can only contemplate it; we cannot comprehend it.

## God Knows Us Continually

Now David contemplates getting away from God; he wonders whether there might be some way to escape the Almighty's continual gaze. Perhaps he feels uncomfortable knowing that God's constant focus is upon him, as if he is the only one in the whole universe.

"Where can I go from your Spirit? Where can I flee from your presence? If I go up to the heavens, you are there; if I make my bed in the depths, you are there" (vv. 7–8). If David reaches to the heavens, of course God is there; if he descends to Sheol, God is there too. Yes, God must of necessity know what is happening in the grave and even in hell. There is no place on the earth or the heavens where God does not see us.

Perhaps David can escape God's observation if he travels to the remotest part of the world: "If I rise on the wings of the dawn, if I settle on the far side of the sea, even there your hand will guide me, your right hand will hold me fast" (vv. 9–10). We marvel at the Old Testament prophet Jonah, who told the sailors that he was running away "from the presence of the LORD" (Jon. 1:10, NASB). That is something we cannot do, for the presence of the Lord is in the remotest region of the sea.

There is one final possibility. What if David takes cover under a blanket of darkness? "If I say, 'Surely the darkness will hide me and the light become night around me,' even the darkness will not be dark to you; the night will shine like the day, for darkness is as light to you" (vv. 11–12). Thieves do their deeds at night, hoping to escape the gaze of men. But to God the darkest night is as bright as the noonday sun. God has no such restrictions or limitations. We commit all our deeds in the blazing sunlight of God's exhaustive knowledge.

## God Knows Us Prophetically

> For you created my inmost being;
> you knit me together in my mother's womb.
> I praise you because I am fearfully and wonderfully made;
> your works are wonderful,
> I know that full well.
> My frame was not hidden from you
> when I was made in the secret place.
> When I was woven together in the depths of the earth,
> your eyes saw my unformed body.
> All the days ordained for me
> were written in your book
> before one of them came to be.
>
> (Ps. 139:13–16)

Before the days of neurology and the unraveling of the DNA code, David already knew that he was a work of unsurpassed wonder. What the world calls a fetus, David would call a preborn infant. Long before our birth, we are known to God, formed according to His will and purpose.

A friend of mine who grew up fatherless in an alcoholic home found comfort in David's words. The fact that it was God who formed him in his mother's womb was of great solace. Perhaps his earthly father did not touch him, but his heavenly Father did.

"All the days ordained for me were written in your book before one of them came to be" (v. 16). Again we must ask: how could all his days be ordained for him before his birth unless God knows the future infallibly? God could not know the number of our days unless He knew our decisions and those of others ahead of time. David understood that God had marvelously planned out his life.

In *Knowing God*, J. I. Packer speaks of the joy and awe God's complete knowledge of us should produce:

> I am graven on the palms of His hands. I am never out of His mind. All my knowledge of Him depends on His sustained initiative in knowing me. I know Him, because He first knew me, and continues to know me. He knows me as a friend, one who loves me; and there is no moment when His eye is off me, or His attention distracted from me, and no moment, therefore, when His care falters.
>
> This is momentous knowledge. There is unspeakable comfort—the sort of comfort that energizes, be it said, not enervates—in knowing that God is constantly taking knowledge of me in love and watching over me for my good. There is tremendous relief in knowing that His love to me is utterly realistic, based at every point on prior knowledge of the worst about me, so that no discovery now can disillusion Him about me, in the way I am so often disillusioned about myself and quench His determination to bless me.[10]

"How precious to me are your thoughts, O God! How vast is the sum of them! Were I to count them, they would outnumber the grains of sand. When I awake, I am still with you" (vv. 17–18). The Lord's thoughts toward David are so priceless, David thinks about them every morning. The fact of God's meticulous interest and knowledge in him is a source of joy and hope.

David now directs his thoughts toward the wicked; he prays that God will judge them. "If only you would slay the wicked, O God! Away from me, you bloodthirsty men!" (v. 19). We are surprised at such language, but remember that David is speaking about people who want to kill him. "Do I not hate those who hate you, O LORD, and abhor those who rise up against you?" (v. 21). The word *hate*, as David uses it here, is akin to our word *reject*; David wants nothing to do with those who hate God. He rejects them and states that if they are God's enemies, they are his enemies too.

David knows that God not only has perfect knowledge of him, but of the wicked too. God will bring them into judgment, and when that happens, He will overlook no fact. They will not have an opportunity to tweak their story or put their spin on events.

But David is wise enough to know that he cannot be satisfied that God knows all things without personally responding to this revelation. He can speak about God's knowledge of facts, he can speak about God's knowledge of the wicked, but the searchlight must now shine into his own soul.

## A PERSONAL RESPONSE

The psalm begins with David saying that God's knowledge of him is an accepted fact; the searching has already taken place. But now he says, "Search me, O God, and know my heart; test me and know my anxious thoughts. See if there is any offensive way in me, and lead me in the way everlasting" (vv. 23–24). He is saying, "God, You have already searched me, and now please show me what You see." That is a brave prayer. We do not want to see what God sees, yet such an experience is the means of healing and benefit.

The more honest we are, the more willing we become to admit that we do not have a clear picture of the lies in our hearts. We are too blind, too spiritually deceitful; we have fooled ourselves too many times to face the sin within. There is much in our hearts that we cannot see unless God reveals it to us. Somewhere I read a story of a woman who said to her pastor, "There is something wrong in my life, and I've asked God to show me what it is; but I have no idea."

He replied, "Just get on your knees and guess at it." Yes, sometimes we know exactly what is within us that displeases the Lord. Other times we must pray like David, "Search me . . . know my heart."

After searching comes testing. "Test me and know my anxious thoughts" (v. 23). Perhaps David is speaking of the anxiety he feels because of the threats of the wicked; he wants to be tested the way a refiner's fire tests metal. And he wants to know whether there is any "offensive" way in him. Perhaps David had a specific sin in mind, perhaps not. Whatever was there, he wanted to see it.

Searching leads to testing and testing leads to leading: "And lead me in the way everlasting" (v. 24). We plead for leading; we don't plead for searching and testing. But perhaps there is an important order here. The leading follows a heart open in God's presence.

Are we willing to pray that prayer?

Yes, God knows whether we will or won't, but His knowledge does not absolve us from responsibility. His exhaustive knowledge should drive us toward Him, not away from Him. Let us say with Peter, "Lord, you know all things; you know that I love you" (John 21:17). For "nothing in all creation is hidden from God's sight. Everything is uncovered and laid bare before the eyes of him to whom we must give account" (Heb. 4:13).

| LIE 8 | The Fall<br>Ruined God's Plan |
|-------|-------------------------------|

WE ALL AGREE THAT SIN RUINED PARADISE. But did it ruin God's eternal plan?

Was God actually expecting, perhaps hoping, that Adam and Eve would obey His command so that they would live in bliss? Or was the whole scheme of sin and redemption in God's mind long before the beautiful fruit of the forbidden tree mesmerized Eve?

Here's how many people see it: God had Plan A, namely, that all of His created beings were to live in obedience and joy. But because these creatures took advantage of their free will, a percentage of the angels and later the entire human race plunged into sin and its ugly consequences. In response, God initiated Plan B, entering the world in the person of Christ to redeem as many people as He could. Thankfully, we are invited to participate in this plan, and of course, we urge others to join us.

In a word, according to this scenario, the fall of man in Eden ruined God's plan. Faced with the reality of the curse, Christ came to clean up the mess. God didn't so much act as *react* to the devastation that sin left in its wake. Like an artist who finds indelible ink spilled by his rival on the original canvas and creatively includes the blotch in his picture, so God took the mess that His rebellious creations handed Him and made the best of it.

This, I believe, is a wrong reading of the Bible's story line. There are compelling reasons to prove that the fall of Lucifer and Adam was Plan

A. The scheme of history and redemption was always in the divine mind; God created that He might redeem; He redeemed that He might better display His glory. Yes, the present world, with all of its sin and pain, is Plan A.

I can hear a chorus of objections: "Didn't Lucifer and Adam and Eve have free will?" "Are all of God's creatures robots, puppets who unknow-ingly follow an invisible, divine blueprint?" Or like one wag put it: "Are you saying that Eve didn't fall but was *pushed*?"

"And what does this say about God—did He will the suffering in the world, the wars, the child abuse, the Holocaust? Can we trust a God who would choose this as the best of all possible worlds? Did He not have better options?"

Another question also arises: "If this is Plan A, does this mean we passively accept this world with all of its evil because everything is God's will anyway? If we fight circumstance, are we not then fighting against God?"

I agree it would be difficult to tell the parents whose children were murdered at Columbine High School that this is Plan A. This world is so obviously out of joint that everyone agrees that things are not as they should be. And yet, as we shall see, only by putting evil within the framework of God's eternal plan do we have any hope that suffering can make any sense at all.

The French writer Voltaire wrote a novel called *Candide*. In this satire, Candide goes from one tragedy to another and keeps telling her-self that this is the "best of all possible worlds." It seemed so obvious to Voltaire that the evils of this world could have no redeemable value that the very idea that this was God's plan seemed unthinkable.

When faced with questions of such sweeping importance, we can-not make personal judgments until we have pondered the biblical data about the nature of God and His purposes. In the last chapter I tried to explain the omniscience of God and its implications. When we under-stand how omniscience combines with omnipotence and wisdom, we cannot believe that things have gone wrong from the divine perspective. Yes, there are terrifying evils in the world; God takes no delight in human suffering; and yet His eternal purposes are on track. Looked at from the standpoint of eternity, this is Plan A.

Before we answer objections, let us meditate on God and His self-revelation. We want to take a brief journey into His mind, trying to understand what He has said about His eternal plan. Join me as we wade into some deep theological waters; so deep, in fact, that at times our feet will not touch bottom. When we emerge I want us to worship God as never before; I want us to see Him as we have never seen Him, and trust Him as we have never trusted Him.

Here we come face to face with the greatness of our God and the mystery that surrounds His purposes. Theology, as we shall see, is to end in doxology; if we probe the mind of God, we shall be led to the praise of God. So let us turn to the Scriptures to make the case that sin, for all of its horror, did not ruin God's eternal plan.

## GOD'S ETERNAL PURPOSES

Try, if you can, to visualize a time when nothing existed but God: no stars, no angels, no worlds, no air, no living beings. Just God, existing in glory and splendor.

We've already emphasized that He did not choose the attributes He has; holiness, power, and mercy were all a part of who He was and is. If He had been sadistic rather than benevolent, we would still have to accept God as He is, and we would have no right to redefine Him according to our terms. Thankfully, He is loving, and so there was fellowship among the members of the Trinity from all of eternity. God was content, not needing anything outside Himself for His pleasure and existence. Paul said, "The God who made the world and everything in it is the Lord of heaven and earth and does not live in temples built by hands. And he is not served by human hands, as if he needed anything, because he himself gives all men life and breath and everything else" (Acts 17:24–25).

If you ask how long God existed before He chose to create, or if you ask what He was doing during those eons, the great theologian Calvin said that He was preparing a hell for people who ask such questions! Just kidding, of course. But we simply don't know the answers since He has not seen fit to reveal them to us. There are some things we know; some things we do not know.

Why then did God create the universe? Perhaps Jonathan Edwards has the best explanation: for the "overflow of his glory." He desired to reveal Himself, to create trillions of stars and a lesser number of planets that would do His bidding to radiate the divine glory and energy.

This thought leads us to the edge of mystery: God did not use any preexisting materials when He spoke everything into existence. Just imagine going into a laboratory with the intention of creating a single molecule out of nothing! It's beyond us, because it is logically evident that from nothing comes nothing. That's true for us, but not for God. He took "nothing" and made "something."

Even creating one thing out of nothing would require omnipotence; only an all-powerful being could accomplish it. And God created all things effortlessly: "By the word of the LORD were the heavens made, their starry host by the breath of his mouth" (Ps. 33:6).

Of course God restrained Himself. He could have created a thousand planets around the sun rather than less than a dozen. He could have created even more stars than the trillions that light up the dark night. He could have created human beings on other planets if that had given him pleasure. It was all His choice. "You are worthy, our Lord and God, to receive glory and honor and power, for you created all things, and by your will they were created and have their being" (Rev. 4:11).

Did God create the devil? Well, not as the devil now is; He did create the angel that became the devil; He created the angels that became the demons. They could not have existed; indeed, they cannot exist today, except by God's sovereign choice and pleasure.

If, however, we ask about God's eternal purpose, the goals He wished His creation to accomplish, the Bible answers this question dozens of times. Creation turns out to be the first link in a chain of providential planning that will encompass all that God wanted to do. And the final link in the chain is always the glory of God.

God, as John Piper likes to point out, is relentlessly self-serving. Everything exists to contribute toward His glory. This does not mean that He is selfish in the usual sense of the word. He must put Himself first because we would expect Him to honor that which is of greatest value, namely, Himself. When we as humans are self-absorbed, we are putting our emphasis on that which is of lesser value, but the creature is never as valuable as the Creator. God has no choice but to put His glory above all else.[1]

Scripture underscores this truth. Declares the Lord God:

I will say to the north, "Give them up!"
  and to the south, "Do not hold them back."
Bring my sons from afar
  and my daughters from the ends of the earth—
everyone who is called by my name,
  *whom I created for my glory,*
  whom I formed and made.

(Isa. 43:6–7, emphasis mine)

Then will all your people be righteous
  and they will possess the land forever.
They are the shoot I have planted,
  the work of my hands,
  *for the display of my splendor.*

(Isa. 60:21, emphasis mine)

"For as a belt is bound around a man's waist, so I bound the whole house of Israel and the whole house of Judah to me," declares the

LORD, "*to be my people for my renown and praise and honor.* But they have not listened."

(Jer. 13:11, emphasis mine)

Yet he saved them *for his name's sake,*
   *to make his mighty power known. . . .*
Then they believed his promises
   and sang his praise.

(Psa. 106:8, 12, emphasis mine)

They will be punished with everlasting destruction and shut out from the presence of the Lord and from the majesty of his power *on the day he comes to be glorified in his holy people and to be marveled at among all whose who have believed.*

(2 Thess. 1:9–10, emphasis mine)

These are just a few of the many passages that stress that all things were created for the glory of God. If you are still not convinced why God created everything, ponder these words: "For by him all things were created: things in heaven and on earth, visible and invisible, whether thrones or powers or rulers or authorities; all things were created by him and for him" (Col. 1:16). Nothing is left out; everything was created *by* Him and *for* Him; let me say it again, *by* Him and *for* Him! *This world was made for Christ.*

With this ultimate goal in mind, God created the angels and the universe with Adam and Eve in Eden. To attain His ultimate goal, He had a host of lesser goals all designed to lead to the final goal. As such all of His purposes are interconnected. Let me give you a contemporary example. When I was in high school, I studied chemistry. Because it was a course I needed to pass, I worked hard to make the grade. But that purpose was part of a larger purpose to graduate from high school, and that purpose led to a more important one, namely, going to Bible college. And even that purpose was really intended to lead me to a more ultimate purpose, namely, to become a preacher and teacher of the Bible. And that purpose leads me to a more important purpose: to see lives changed by the power of the gospel.

Just so, all the purposes of God form a connected system, with one event existing for the next event that grows out of it. The creation of the world led to the creation of Adam and Eve; the birth of their children led to other purposes and so it has been throughout the ages. As for the angels, God created them for a purpose that would lead to other purposes, all of which will contribute to God's glory.

Our intentions are often frustrated because of lack of knowledge. You might want to buy your wife flowers on the way home, but when you stop at the shop you discover that it has gone out of business. Or, much to your surprise, the fifty dollars you thought you had in your wallet was removed by your teenager, who forgot to tell you that he took the money when you were taking a shower because he was desperate to pay for a college textbook.

One day I stopped at a hospital to visit a friend, not knowing that he had already died. My "foreknowledge" was not foreknowledge at all. On another occasion my wife and I planned to go on a cruise only to discover it had to be canceled because the ship needed unexpected repairs. Thanks to how little I know, my plans have to be constantly revised.

But God has no such contingencies. "Known unto God are all his works from the beginning of the world" (Acts 15:18, KJV).

Let us think about this carefully. First, God is *omnipotent;* that is, He is all-powerful. There is nothing He cannot do except violate His own nature. He could even have created creatures who would always obey Him. Yes, He could have created a host of creatures like the good angels who even now do His bidding. Or, for that matter, He could have created us as we will be in heaven: perfect, with neither the desire nor the ability to sin. All those options, plus a host of others, were before Him.

Second, God is *omniscient.* Nothing will happen that will catch Him by surprise. When He created Lucifer, God knew that he would sin;

when He created Adam, He knew that he would fall. No new fact can ever arise that God did not take into account; no creature can make a choice of which God was not aware. "But God made the earth by his power; he founded the world by his wisdom and stretched out the heavens by his understanding" (Jer. 10:12). God's omnipotence and omniscience are linked.

Omniscience, as we have learned, means that everything was foreknown. And since God's knowledge was not faulty, He knew the future would turn out just as He saw it before Him. Knowing what He knew, God could have chosen to create an entirely different world: a world without a devil, a world with people whose hearts were always inclined to do what was right. His options were beyond our imagination.

Third, God is *omnipresent;* He fills the universe. This means that there is no place where God is not. Nothing can happen behind His back; no plot can be hatched in some smoke-filled room from which He is barred. Go to the far reaches of space, and God is there. "'Can anyone hide in secret places so that I cannot see him?' declares the LORD. 'Do not I fill heaven and earth?'" (Jer. 23:24).

Notice how His attributes are often combined in Scripture: Jeremiah connected God's omnipotence and wisdom: "But God made the earth by his power; he founded the world by his wisdom and stretched out the heavens by his understanding" (Jer. 10:12). Also, omnipresence and omniscience are connected. When God acts, all of His attributes act in concert; none acts independently; none diminishes the other.

Now it is time for a personal question: do you think that this God— who is so powerful, so filled with knowledge and wisdom—would have created a universe in which something might happen contrary to His will? I think not. Job was right when he said, "I know that you can do all things; no plan of yours can be thwarted" (Job 42:2). Not even free will can stand in the way of God's ultimate purposes. God's power, knowledge, and wisdom are infinite.

Listen to the words of Charles Alexander:

If God were less than omnipotent, or if He allowed evil to develop and multiply itself in His own domain of creation without His prior decree and permission, and purpose, then He is not God, and cannot be God. If evil there must be, let us be in the hands of God and not of chance, for if evil comes from outside the divine decree, otherwise than by the will of God, then there must be another god beside God.[2]

Creation was the first major link in the connectedness of God's purposes. But long before creation, the death of Christ, the salvation of His people, and the triumph of Christ over evil were already in the divine mind. Creation was the outworking in time of the eternal plan.

## GOD'S ETERNAL REDEMPTION

Paul shows the connection between creation and redemption: "For he chose us in him [Christ] before the creation of the world to be holy and blameless in his sight" (Eph. 1:4). Paul refers to the creation of the world but says that something had already happened prior to the earth's birth. Before the worlds were spun into existence, before Adam and Eve walked among the trees of Eden, the plan of redemption was in God's mind. Already, then, He had chosen a group of people to be holy and blameless. We cannot think of creation apart from redemption; the two were linked, from the beginning, in the mind of God. "The world was made for Calvary; when God created the world it was with the intention of dying for it. The remedy was in advance of the disease."[3]

I know of a pastor who believes that God had high hopes for Adam and Eve, but they disappointed Him. So He turned to Plan B. In a message titled "God the Gambler," this man said that God gambled on mankind, betting that they would serve Him. When He lost the gamble, He did what any gambler does: He upped the ante and bet His only Son. This pastor actually rephrased John 3:16: "For God so loved the world that He *bet* His only begotten Son."

For this minister, if we dare call him such, there were no guarantees; God had no assurance that anyone would believe on Christ after He died for sinners. After all, because of free will it was conceivable that no one would believe on Christ. God could have lost the whole gamble! According to this scenario, the death of Christ was God's response to an emergency He was hoping would not happen. We can be grateful that God chose to clean up the mess, but He lost the game. Nothing about His plans was certain. Yet because God is loving, we can expect Him to do whatever He can to help us.

How demeaning!

Needless to say, the cross of Christ was a planned event from all eternity. Although I quoted these verses earlier in this book, I repeat them here. "This man," said Peter in the Book of Acts, "was handed over to you *by God's set purpose* and foreknowledge; and you, with the help of wicked men, put him to death by nailing him to the cross" (Acts 2:23, emphasis mine). And again, "Indeed Herod and Pontius Pilate met together with the Gentiles and the people of Israel in this city to conspire against your holy servant Jesus, whom you anointed. *They did what your power and will had decided beforehand should happen*" (Acts 4:27–28, emphasis mine).

God planned the cross in the distant eons of eternity because He planned our redemption before He created us. "[God] has saved us, and called us with a holy calling, not according to our works, but according to His own purpose and grace which was granted us in Christ Jesus *from all eternity*" (2 Tim. 1:9, NASB, emphasis mine). Literally, the Greek text reads that grace was granted to us "before the ages of eternity"!

Perhaps, however, the clearest text that shows that God created that He might redeem is in Ephesians, where Paul says that he was called to preach to the Gentiles the unsearchable riches of Christ, which for ages were "kept hidden in God, who created all things. His intent was that now, through the church, the manifold wisdom of God should be made known to the rulers and authorities in the heavenly realms, *according to his eternal purpose which he accomplished in Christ Jesus our Lord"* (Eph. 3:9–11, emphasis mine).

Don't miss the connection: the God who created all things planned that the church show forth His wisdom, and this was His "eternal purpose"! No wonder we cannot separate creation from redemption. God's first purpose was to redeem, and creation was the necessary step to accomplish it. Without creation, there would have been no redeemed creatures to display His glory; without a church, His manifold wisdom in salvation would not have been exhibited. The world was created *"by* Him and *for* Him."

However much we struggle with the fact that God has no beginning, we can rejoice that He has known the redeemed as long as He has existed. For untold eons, He knew He would grant us grace. To put it differently, if you are redeemed, there never was a time when God did not already love you, when you were not the object of His specific purpose. That is why John could say that our names were written in the Lamb's Book of Life "from the foundation of the world" (Rev. 13:8, NASB).

Understandably, we struggle when we speak of God choosing, willing, and planning from all eternity. What is important is that we realize that there was a cross in God's heart long before there was a cross raised upon the mount of Calvary. God left nothing in His universe to chance; He made no gamble here.

If you, dear reader, think that you might have been left out of God's plan; if you wonder whether you are among the chosen, those whom God foreknew as His from all eternity, let me encourage you. You can find out whether God granted you grace from all eternity. Simply come to Christ and receive Him by faith; transfer all of your trust to Him for your eternal salvation. He has promised to receive you; your desire to belong to Him is good reason to believe that He has drawn you to Himself (John 1:12).

Although creation preceded redemption in time, it is redemption that was uppermost in God's mind. Creation set the stage for redemption;

it was a necessary link to display the eternal purpose. And now the third link in the chain will make God's purposes even clearer.

## GOD'S FUTURE CONSUMMATION

We've emphasized that God created all things for His glory. And now we come to the purpose of it all: "And he made known to us the mystery of his will according to his good pleasure, which he purposed in Christ, to be put into effect when the times will have reached their fulfillment—to bring all things in heaven and on earth together under one head, even Christ" (Eph. 1:9–10).

Paul refers to "when the times will have reached their fulfillment," that is, when all the eras of this earth will have passed away. Historians speak of the various ages, the prehistoric ages, the Dark Ages, the Middle Ages, the Age of Aquarius. One purpose will blend into another until the will of God is completely accomplished. And when it all is over, all things will be unified under the authority of Christ—not Buddha, not Muhammad, but Christ.

Left to themselves, most things fall apart rather than come together. Disintegration is a part of our natural observation of things; nature drifts toward randomness. The universe, we are told, is still expanding. God will put an end to all this disunity and bring everything under Christ's banner. There is nothing loose on planet earth, nothing out of control, nothing that is left to random forces or chance. God holds the cards. The certainty of His purposes should cause us to rejoice.

There is a story about a man who visited a rug factory. While standing on the floor and looking up, he could see the bottom of a huge rug that was being sewn at a higher level. The strings were tangled and knotted. The different colored threads crisscrossed in unrelated patterns. But then as he ascended a ladder and saw the top of the rug, he was amazed at its impressive designs and symmetry. The beauty of its colors and the details of the handiwork captivated his attention.

We look at life from the bottom up. We insist that there must be some mistake; surely something has gotten out of hand; the Weaver could not possibly find a design in the senseless evils of this world. Nothing, we think, could justify the suffering found on this planet. But the beautiful pattern on the side we cannot see is a picture of God's beloved Son. His plan is on target.

## QUESTIONS ABOUT GOD'S GREAT PLAN

So was the Garden of Eden just a setup, a stage for the puppets called Adam and Eve? And Lucifer—what choice did he have if all of this was God's plan? And could the Holocaust have been avoided if everything happens in conformity to the divine plan? Can we trust a God who willed that evil be a part of what He intended to accomplish? These questions need answers.

### The Question of Free Will

There is a story about a group of theologians who were discussing the doctrines of predestination and free will. When the argument became heated, the dissidents split into two groups. One man, unable to make up his mind which group to join, slipped into the predestination crowd. Challenged as to why he was there, he replied, "I came of my own free will."

"Free will! You don't belong here!" the predestinarians retorted.

So he retreated to the opposing "free will" group; and when asked why he switched, he responded, "I was sent here."

"Get out," they stormed. "You can't join us unless you come of your own free will." The confused man was left out in the cold.

The relationship between God's will and man's will has been the subject of debate for centuries, and I would not pretend to solve the mystery in a few paragraphs. In fact, not all theologians define the term *free will* in the same way. In the space of a few paragraphs, I can only point the direction such a discussion should go.

God created us with wills that act on the basis of our inclinations, desires, or knowledge; we are unaware of a divine decree. If you had asked Pilate why he allowed Christ to be put to death, he would not have said, "Because God has convinced me that this is what I should do." He acted according to his desires; yet, as we have already seen, Peter pointed out that Pilate and the other conspirators committed acts that God predetermined would take place. "They did what your power and will had decided beforehand should happen" (Acts 4:28).

God has arranged the universe so that our desires converge with His purposes. Interestingly, the Bible does not see a contradiction between human responsibility and divine providence and direction. The same scripture that teaches that Christ died by the predetermined will of God also calls the men who carried it out wicked; they are accountable for their actions (Acts 2:23).

Perhaps the best I can do in this context is to simply say this: any view of free will that denies that God rules among the inhabitants of the earth is unscriptural; any view of predestination that makes us into puppets is equally unscriptural. The Bible presents a convergence between our inclinations, desires, and choices and the will and plan of God. These come together to accomplish His purposes. God's side renders the events certain; our side means that we act responsibly. Elsewhere I have written on this topic in greater detail.[4]

## The Question of God's Will

How can we say that evil is "the will of God"? Is it not plain that evil is *contrary* to the will of God? How could this wicked world be Plan A? The horrendous suffering in Armenia, Kosovo, and Rwanda, God's will?

We must distinguish between God's revealed will (which is not being done on earth) and His hidden will. Certainly the evil of this world violates all that God has revealed about the value of human life, the need for kindness, and the essentiality of moral purity. God has revealed His laws, which are constantly broken on planet earth, and several passages spell out in detail the will of God for the Christian (Rom. 12:2; 1 Thess. 4:3, 5:18). But, as Luther pointed out, there is a hidden will of God that is always being carried out; this secret will is not something we can question but just one more reason to stand in awe of God.

We can find evidence of this overarching, secret will of God in many places in Scripture. God commanded Abraham to sacrifice Isaac, yet the Almighty had secretly planned that the boy would live (Gen. 22). God commanded Moses to tell Pharaoh to let the people go, but secretly God planned that Pharaoh's heart would be hardened so that he would not obey Moses (Exod. 4:21). Perhaps the clearest evidence of such a hidden will is in Romans 9, a chapter that I encourage you to read and ponder. When the saints in Rome thought that God's will was failing, Paul reassured them that the Almighty's eternal purposes were on track. It is the Potter who "has mercy on whom he wants to have mercy, and he hardens whom he wants to harden" (v.18). It is the Potter who uses "objects of his wrath . . . to make the riches of his glory known to the objects of his mercy, whom he prepared in advance for glory" (vv. 22–23).

Somewhere I read this story that illustrates how God's secret will is being done: Suppose there was a nobleman with an estate covered with trees. He loved his trees, calling each by name, taking proper care of them. Unfortunately, he had an enemy who wanted to hurt him in the worst possible way. So one night, the evil man scaled the fence and cut down what he believed was the nobleman's favorite tree; unfortunately for him, he was so excited he ran the wrong way and the tree fell on him, pinning him to the ground.

Shortly after daybreak, the evil man saw the nobleman and another man walking toward him. He knew he would be caught, but the fact that he had cut down the nobleman's favorite tree filled him with delight. "I ruined your favorite tree," he said in a choked whisper.

The nobleman looked at the pathetic man and said, "The man with me today is a building contractor. I knew I needed to cut down a tree to build myself a summer house, and I came to show the contractor which tree it would be. Thank you for doing the work for me." (Of course, the man was appropriately judged for his evil deed, though it fit the noble-man's plan beautifully.)

Is God's revealed will always being done on earth? No, evil men are doing terrible things, insulting the Almighty. And yet no matter what evil men do, it advances the eternal plan of God; and in the end, writes Charles Alexander, "Evil shall be seen to have been the slave of provi-dence to introduce a higher and greater good than ever could have been, had there been no evil at all."[5] This is surely what Paul meant when he said we were predestined "according to the plan of him who works out everything in conformity with the purpose of his will" (Eph. 1:11). Thus the creatures' rebellion keeps promoting the will and the purposes of the Creator.

## The Question of Conflict

If the world is running according to God's plan, does this mean that we passively accept evil because all that happens is God's will? No, we are not passive because we believe that it is God's revealed will that we fight against evil wherever we find it. As we have already learned about natu-ral disasters, *evil is given to us in order that we might glorify God by over-coming it.* We honor God when we wage war against the world, the flesh, and the devil.

It was easy for Voltaire to write a satire about this being "the best of all possible worlds." Obviously this is not; injustice and cruelty of every sort abound. However, from God's perspective, at work is the best of all possible *plans.* "If God would concede me His omnipotence for twenty-four hours, you would see how many changes I would make in the world," wrote J. Monsabre. "But if He gave me His wisdom too, *I would leave things as they are*" (emphasis mine).[6] Well said.

This is not the best of all possible planets, but from the standpoint of eternity, the best of all possible Architects chose the best of all possi-ble blueprints. Come to think of it, would a good, omnipotent God choose anything less than the best? The fact that this is Plan A does not mean that God is pleased with the injustice and suffering on this planet, nor should we be. Yes, Plan A includes evil, but it also includes eventual success in the struggle against it. It includes eternity, not just time.

An illustration might help. Is painful heart surgery the best of all possible experiences? My friend who just had such surgery, and suffered greatly, would shout *no!* Yet if we look at it from the longer point of view, the answer is *yes,* for the surgery is the means to a longer life and better health.

Christians should be on the forefront, fighting for an end to racism, the rescue of the poor, and the protection of unborn children. Above all we should be willing to follow the lead of our Savior and give our lives for others. The eventual triumph of God's justice, love, and sovereign rule is an indispensable aspect of Plan A; so we rebuke the devil; we fight with the armor of God; we stand against injustice; we identify ourselves with the suffering of humanity, even as Christ did. We are not satisfied with the status quo. We dedicate ourselves to making this world a better place.

Those who use God's sovereignty as an excuse for lack of direct action in the battle against the devil have failed to maintain the biblical balance. They forget that God's sovereign will includes the conflict between good and evil and God is glorified when we identify ourselves with Him in the conflict.

### The Question of Trust

Can God be trusted?

Let us take that question to Kosovo and ask a child whose parents were killed in a civil war. Let us ask the Jews who survived the concentration camps whether a good God chose the best plan for this world. Let us talk to parents whose children are suffering from a dozen different diseases whether they think God's plan is good. Let us ask the children who are being abused today whether God's plan is right and just.

Could not God have chosen a world with a bit more care? Can we trust a God whose plan included such pain for so many and for millions the judgment of an eternal hell?

Yes, we can trust Him.

In fact, the only reason we can trust Him is because we know that He is in charge, and therefore there must be a good reason to allow evil to enter the world. He must have had a good purpose in including it as part of His eternal plan. In fact, only a God for whom there is no risk is trustworthy. Only because His sovereignty extends to every part of history can we be confident that each evil will be exchanged for some higher good.

So we face a choice: either we have a God who stands by as an interested bystander, limited in what He can do because His creatures have free will; or we have a God for whom this world is Plan A. If you choose the latter, you can have confidence that every single detail on this planet has meaning; every evil must be answered with divine justice; every good must be rewarded according to its value. *We can be confident that there must be a morally sufficient reason for evil, even if that reason is known to God alone.*

Perhaps you object to what I have written in this chapter, insisting that the fall of man did, in fact, ruin God's intended plan. If so, the consequences are frightening. I would find it difficult to trust a God who had to switch to a Plan B because Plan A was thwarted. If something happened that was actually beyond His plan, then other unplanned things might happen in the future. I can much better trust a God who from the beginning had a plan that even today is on target. Someday God might explain to us how the senseless evils of life did in fact make sense from His divine point of view. You see, to diminish God's control does not increase my faith; the greater His control, the greater my faith that He will bring it all to completion. Only if God reigns over all things do I have hope.

To put it clearly, senseless evil has a purpose only if it is a part of God's plan. A plane carrying a crew of people intent on helping the refugees in a war-torn country crashes; does God not care about the needy refugees? After the earthquake in Turkey, rains came, making survivors' efforts to find relatives and to take care of themselves more difficult. A judge gives custody of a child to an abusing husband because of a bribe. There are thousands of such events, which from our standpoint are senseless and evil. Yet if this fallen world is a part of God's plan, we can be sure that there must be a purpose in it all. Not a single event happens that will not be used for some justifiable end.

Darrell Scott, whose daughter, Rachel, was murdered in the Columbine High School massacre, knows this truth. He does not seethe with anger. According to *Time* magazine, Darrell and his family have found deliverance from despair. "To them, Rachel's death was a Christian martyrdom—*an act of God* meant to spark a spiritual revolution in young people" (emphasis mine).[7] Needless to say, God does not commit evil, but if the death of Christ was "an act of God" carried out by wicked men, the death of a young woman carried out by wicked teenagers can be described in the same way. Only if God is sovereign do we have the hope that the evils of this world will further God's purposes.

One day I was mowing the lawn when I noticed the fragment of a letter that had blown onto our yard. I was able to read several sentences of it; it described a failed friendship between the author and the addressee. I understood a bit of what had gone on, but quite frankly, I couldn't get the whole picture. What I needed was the rest of the letter, the details of the beginning and the conclusion. I needed context.

Just so with God's purposes. We have His Word, which is reliable but incomplete. We have enough knowledge for faith but not for sight. We have enough understanding to live but not to explain. In this life we have one scene in a drama, but we do not yet see the whole play. We know who wins, but we don't know the whys and the wherefores. We could ask a hundred questions and the Bible would remain silent. As Charles Swindoll says, belief in the sovereignty of God "does not take away my questions, but it does relieve me of anxiety."[8]

Here we bow before our Maker, humbly admitting that there is much about Him that we do not know. God has a right to reveal only a part of His will. All that we can say is that He has revealed Himself as sovereign, loving, and wise. Yes, we would have done it differently, but as the Bible says, God does not have counselors with whom He discusses His next move. We can only rejoice that He makes all of His decisions with ultimately loving and righteous intentions.

What if God wanted a company of people who would trust Him even though His ways are "past finding out"? What if His desire was to have us believe that He is good, though there appears to be so much evidence to the contrary? Faced with God's inscrutable ways, Peter wrote, "In this you greatly rejoice, though now for a little while you may have had to suffer grief in all kinds of trials. These have come so that your faith—of greater worth than gold, which perishes even though refined by fire—may be proved genuine and may result in praise, glory and honor when Jesus Christ is revealed" (1 Pet. 1:6–7).

Finally, we must fall at God's feet in worship. The Bible opens with the declaration "In the beginning God created the heavens and the earth" (Gen. 1:1). Near its close we read, "The Lord our God, the Almighty, reigns" (Rev. 19:6, NASB). Between those pages is the assurance that we serve a God who does all things well.

## A PERSONAL RESPONSE

Let's pretend that we are in heaven looking back to planet earth and the drama that was played out there, spanning thousands of years. We are impressed with how tiny the earth is, silhouetted against the vast expanse of the myriad of stars in the distant heavens. And yet, on that speck, the struggle between evil and good, light and darkness came to its glorious conclusion. With the angels we shout,

> Amen!
> Praise and glory
> and wisdom and thanks and honor
> and power and strength

be to our God for ever and ever.

Amen!

(Rev. 7:12)

Only then will we understand that God did all things well.

Until then, we rejoice in worship, believing that God's will and ways are just and good. When Paul discussed the ultimate purposes of God, he ended with a breathtaking doxology, reminding us we can see only a glimmer of God's ultimate plans. We adore Him both for what we know and the mysteries we cannot fathom. His ways, says Paul, are "beyond tracing out."

> Oh, the depth of the riches of the wisdom
>> and knowledge of God!
>> How unsearchable his judgments,
>> and his paths beyond tracing out!
> "Who has known the mind of the Lord?
>> Or who has been his counselor?"
> "Who has ever given to God,
>> that God should repay him?"
> For from him and through him and to him
>> are all things.
> To him be the glory forever!
>> Amen!

(Rom. 11:33–36)

Let's ponder those last lines. "For *from* him [creation] and *through* him [redemption] and *to* him [consummation] are all things."

Yes, to Him be glory forever—amen!

# LIE 9 | We Must Choose between God's Pleasures and Our Own

At Moody Church we interview prospective deacons to evaluate their fitness for office. Our constitution requires that we ask a number of questions, including this one: "Are you opposed, both in theory and practice, to indulgence in all questionable or sensual amusements that mar your fellowship with Christ?" One candidate replied, "Yes, I do oppose these things. In fact, my marriage is very boring."

Though others might have put it more diplomatically, he reflected the mind-set of many misinformed Christians: either we seek our own pleasures or we give God pleasure by our obedience, but we cannot do both. The choice is between personal happiness and duty, freedom or drudgery. Indeed, one Christian man told me that he didn't buy a sweater simply because he liked it. Sometimes this man would say, "There is something wrong with me: I have not cried in a while." For him all pleasure was sin; endless self-mortification and boredom were the keys to the Christian life.

"Because I live only once, I figure I should get all the happiness I can," another young man told me. I tried to help him understand that his lifestyle of drinking and immorality was leading nowhere; he should accept Christ as Savior and be reconciled to God. But the very suggestion that he turn from his pleasures to God was unthinkable. What was he to do? Sit home and watch reruns of pre-1964 movies? Why should he exchange his delights for dullness? God, he thought, would put an end to his joy.

"Can't I live the good life and then accept Christ just before I die?" asked an alcoholic. He also thought that accepting Christ as Savior meant that he would transition from "the good life" to something far less. To trade in his bottle for God meant he would be shortchanged.

The purpose of this chapter is to show that God has pleasures and so should we. The Bible does not deny us enjoyment; in fact, it commands us to seek the highest pleasures: "Delight yourself in the LORD and he will give you the desires of your heart" (Ps. 37:4). Our desires are not to be despised, but fulfilled. I hope to show that in seeking God's pleasures we will be seeking our own. Thankfully, the choice is not between putting ourselves or God first. *When we put God first, we put ourselves first!*

I'm indebted to two books by John Piper *Desiring God* and *The Pleasures of God* for many of the insights found in this chapter. I commend these books to you for study and reflection.[1] A conclusion I've reached based on my study of these books is that we can study the doctrine of God, but at the end of the day, it is our desire for Him and seeking of Him that must be the goal of our knowledge.

## FIVE LINKS IN THE CHAIN OF JOY

If we are to seek our pleasure in God, He cannot give us happiness unless it is His to give. Thankfully, He is a God of pleasure, and He wants us to follow His example. The following five statements are links in a chain leading us to personal happiness and fulfillment. They show that our quest for meaning and happiness is rooted in the very nature of God. To believe that knowing God leads to boredom is about as far from the truth as one can travel.

Note: don't draw any conclusions from any one of these links in the chain of joy until you see how they are connected. We shall root joy in the character of God as a basis for our own spiritual pleasures. One truth builds upon another until we see more clearly that we give God pleasure when we find our own pleasure in Him.

## God Himself Has Many Pleasures

"It is good news that God is gloriously happy," writes John Piper. "No one would want to spend eternity with an unhappy God."[2] The uncontrollable twists and turns of life often frustrate our desire for happiness. The job we chose was not what we were told it would be; the partner we marry is diagnosed with a disease whose name we cannot pronounce; our vacation was cut short by a tornado. Daily we are reminded that our best-laid plans are subject to a dozen different unforeseen happenstances.

Now for a moment, imagine, as best you can, what it would be like to be God. You are all-powerful, so nothing can defeat you; you are all-knowing, so nothing can outwit you; you are all-present, so nothing can outlast you. Clearly, you have all the resources needed to be happy!

Add to this wisdom, goodness, glory, and beauty, and you can see that God's desires are never frustrated. "Our God is in heaven; he does whatever pleases him" (Ps. 115:3). Imagine being able to do whatever you want to do! No wonder He is happy!

In what does God take delight? First of all, in His Son: "This is my Son, whom I love; with him I am well pleased. Listen to him!" (Matt. 17:5). Isaiah quotes God as saying, "Here is my servant, whom I uphold, my chosen one in whom I delight" (Isa. 42:1). Paul echoes God's joy in His Son, "For God was pleased to have all his fullness dwell in him" (Col. 1:19).

The Father's delight in the Son has existed as long as God has existed and will exist forever. "If there is any enthusiasm in God . . . it is his enthusiasm for the Son. It will never change; it will never cool off. It burns with unimaginable fervency and zeal."[3] Jonathan Edwards was right when he said, "The infinite happiness of the Father consists in the enjoyment of His Son." As we have learned, God has not revealed what He was doing before the worlds were created, but of this we can be certain: He was enjoying the Son, and they were fellowshipping together with great mutual satisfaction.

Second, God delights in His creation. "God saw all that he had made, and it was very good" (Gen. 1:31). He was satisfied with the work He had so easily accomplished. The psalmist knows that the glory of the Lord endures forever and prays that the Lord might "rejoice in his works" (Ps. 104:31).

God asked Job whether he understood what it took to create the world: "On what were its footings set, or who laid its cornerstone—while the morning stars sang together and all the angels shouted for joy?" (Job 38:6–7). Apparently God created the angels before He created the universe so that there would be an audience for the event. Imagine the exuberance of the angels when the galaxies floated into existence! If these beings get their dispositions from their Father, we can be sure that the Almighty was rejoicing along with them. John Piper says we can almost imagine God saying, "Watch this!" and the heavenly hosts burst out in rapturous applause.[4]

When God gave the commandment, "You shall have no other gods before me" (Exod. 20:3), this law also applied to Himself. If He were to find His chief delight in any other creature or even His own creation, He would be guilty of idolatry; so His delight is rooted in Himself. But He can rejoice in His creation because it expresses His glory: "The heavens declare the glory of God; the skies proclaim the work of his hands. Day after day they pour forth speech; night after night they display knowledge" (Ps. 19:1–2). Day and night the creation shouts, "God is glorious; God is glorious!"

God also rejoices in His works of creation because they praise Him (Ps. 103:22). In fact, the marine life He created praises Him in "all ocean depths" (Ps. 148:7). He delights in the hidden secrets of the sea, even if man should never discover them.

The Father and the Son cooperated in creation (Col. 1:16). No deficiency in them caused them to create; the universe was the expression of their mutual joy. "The Son and the Father are equally glorified in creation, because creation is the overflow of gladness that they have in each other."[5]

Just as God rejoices in creation, so can we. The essence of idolatry is to substitute the creature for the Creator, but we are not idolaters if we see creation as an expression of God's glory and power. Having seen the marvels of what God has made stimulates us to consider: if the creation is glorious, think of the greater glory of the Creator!

God also delights in His people. "He guides me in paths of right-eousness for his name's sake" (Ps. 23:3). God's primary reason for His personal investment in the lives of His people is His reputation. Affirms John Piper, "God's first love is rooted in the value of his holy name, not the value of sinful people."[6] Yet He delights in doing good to His people: "The LORD your God is with you, he is mighty to save. He will take great delight in you, he will quiet you with his love, he will rejoice over you with singing" (Zeph. 3:17). Again, God rejoices in us because we bring glory to Him. He is relentlessly self-seeking because there is no one beyond Him to whom He owes His existence or success.

God finds much in which He can delight.

But is He always happy? Isn't there much in the world that makes Him grieve? Many passages speak of God as being angry. In fact, "God is a righteous judge, a God who expresses his wrath every day" (Ps. 7:11). Some things give Him no delight: "Do I take any pleasure in the death of the wicked? declares the Sovereign LORD. Rather, am I not pleased when they turn from their ways and live? . . . For I take no pleasure in the death of anyone, declares the Sovereign LORD" (Ezek. 18:23, 32). Verse 32 forces us to question whether God might always be pleased or not; if some events trouble Him, is He *cornered* into unhappiness?[7]

John Piper finds the answer in the "infinitely complex emotional life of God." In one sense God is grieved by the death of the wicked, the rebellion of mankind. But when He considers all of the events that have led up to such rebellion and what will flow from it, He is pleased. Moses warned of the coming judgment and said, "Just as it pleased the LORD to make you prosper and increase in number, so it will please him to ruin and destroy you" (Deut. 28:63). Interestingly, the same psalm that assures us that "the LORD does whatever pleases him" describes how God struck down the Egyptians as well as "mighty kings" (Ps. 135:6–12); such judgments give Him pleasure because of His desire for justice and righteous condemnation. In short, God is never trapped or forced to do something that does not please Him; at the end of the day, all of His works give Him pleasure.[8]

God is a happy God.

### God Created Us to Seek Pleasure

It would be strange indeed if our Creator enjoyed pleasures but denied them to us! Can we imagine our Father in heaven rejoicing while telling us that we must not seek our own enjoyment? He created us to seek pleasure; indeed, we cannot act otherwise.

Perhaps no one wrote more convincingly about our frustration in trying to find happiness than Blaise Pascal. Despite our relentless quest, we do not find the happiness we seek in those things that hold out the promise of fulfillment. Speaking of human nature, he wrote: "It wants to be great and sees that it is only small. It wants to be happy and finds it is wretched. It wants to be perfect and sees itself full of imperfections. It wants to be the object of other people's love and esteem and sees that its faults deserve only their dislike and contempt."[9] Our problem is not that we seek happiness, but that we seek it in all the wrong places.

Pascal continued, "All look for happiness without exception. Although they use different means, they all strive toward this objective. That is why some go to war and some do other things. So this is the motive for every deed of man, including those who hang themselves."[10] The present, he contended, can never satisfy us; though our present experience promises fulfillment, we are deceived by following one false path after another until death finally claims us. Please keep in mind that Pascal was not saying that we should not seek happiness; indeed, it is necessary that we do so. But as we shall see, our thirst for happiness must lead to the right object.

C. S. Lewis echoed the same thoughts, asserting that our desire for happiness is something God actually gave us.

If there lurks in most modern minds the notion that to desire our own good and earnestly hope for the enjoyment of it is a bad thing, I submit that this notion has crept in from Kant and the Stoics and is not part of the Christian faith. Indeed, if we consider the unblushing promises of reward and the staggering nature of the rewards promised in the Gospels, it would seem that our Lord finds our desires not too strong but too weak. We are halfhearted creatures, fooling about with drink and sex and ambition when infinite joy is offered us, like an ignorant child who wants to go on making mud pies in a slum because he cannot imagine what is meant by the offer of a holiday at the sea. We are far too easily pleased.[11]

No one seeks wretchedness. I have performed many marriages but have never heard a bride or groom say, "We are getting married because we want to be miserable." Even those who know that they should not marry do so because they believe that the pain of living alone will be greater than the pain of the marriage. And yes, Pascal is right: the person who commits suicide does so because he believes that the pain on the other side of the grave will be less than the present grief.

Think of ways in which we try to minimize pain and maximize pleasure. We submit to surgery, hoping it will eventually help us feel better, and if we choose a vocation we don't like, it is because we believe that the meager salary it brings will make us happier than if we starved to death. The man who commits immorality does so because he thinks it will maximize pleasure if he can minimize the pain by keeping it secret. The dedicated Sunday school teacher prepares his lesson well because he believes this will bring the most happiness and benefit to his students; furthermore, he has the satisfaction of a job well done. Whether Christians, Muslims, Jews, or atheists, we all seek to avoid pain and increase our pleasure.

God, who seeks pleasure, created us so that we might do the same. Created in His image, we seek our own interests; we calculate what is best for us. God, however, is not led astray, and we are.

### Our Temptation Is to Seek Lesser Pleasures

When Adam and Eve were in the Garden they enjoyed two special kinds of pleasures: knowing God and walking with Him. There was also the temptation of the pleasure of eating from the forbidden tree. "When the woman saw that the fruit of the tree was good for food and pleasing to the eye, and also desirable for gaining wisdom, she took some and ate it" (Gen. 3:6). The tree was good, because everything God created was good. The problem was that God had told them not to eat of it. Our first parents faced a choice: what would bring them the most pleasure? In their minds, eating would bring more pleasure than not eating. Gaining wisdom would be more delightful than not gaining any. But because they could not foresee the consequences of disobedience, they brought much unhappiness to themselves and to the world. The disobedience they thought would increase their happiness instead maximized their pains.

Like Adam and Eve, Moses also sought pleasure, but he chose to find it in obedience. "By faith Moses, when he had grown up, refused to be known as the son of Pharaoh's daughter. He chose to be mistreated along with the people of God rather than to enjoy the pleasures of sin for a short time. He regarded disgrace for the sake of Christ as of greater value than the treasures of Egypt, because he was looking ahead to his reward" (Heb. 11:24–26).

Moses calculated his options: *Should I seek the pleasures of sin, or the pleasures of God, the "eternal reward"?* Either way, he was motivated by what was best for him, what would give him the most delight. So he turned from the fleeting pleasures of sin and chose the lasting pleasures that come to all those who follow God's way.

Jesus did the same. "Let us fix our eyes on Jesus, the author and perfecter of our faith, who for the joy set before him endured the cross,

TEN LIES ABOUT GOD

scorning its shame, and sat down at the right hand of the throne of God" (Heb. 12:2). Jesus knew that the future joy would be greater than the present pain. Yes, He could have called myriads of angels, and they would have delivered Him from His present grief; but He would have missed the greater joy that followed His obedience.

When we choose the lesser pleasures, we substitute the creation for the Creator. We can quickly become idolaters, worshiping the temporary delights of life instead of eternal God. Both the pleasures of this world and the pleasures of God make the same promise; both court our allegiance. But the lesser pleasures cannot deliver on their promises.

How can we describe worldly pleasures? They are fragile, insubstantial; they evaporate the moment we think they are within our grasp. D. L. Moody, who founded the church where I serve as senior pastor, had a favorite verse that contrasted two different kinds of pleasure: "The world and its desires pass away, but the man who does the will of God lives forever" (1 John 2:17). Even if we can eke out a few years of worldly pleasure, gratifying whatever desires we wish, they will not last. Robert Burns was right:

> Pleasures are like poppies spread,—
> You seize the flower, its bloom is shed
> Or like the snowfalls in the river—
> A moment white, then melts forever.[12]

These delights also purport to take the place of God. But they do not perform up to expectation. Luther was correct when he said, "No man sins, but that he thinks wrongly about God." Certainly Adam and Eve would not have sinned if they had believed that God was good. Sensual pleasures say, "God doesn't meet my needs! God doesn't meet my needs!" To quote Piper once more, "Sin is what we do when we are not satisfied with God; it holds out the promise of happiness."[13]

Finally, these pleasures promise freedom, but they bring slavery. Let us hear it from Jesus: "I tell you the truth, everyone who sins is a slave to sin. Now a slave has no permanent place in the family, but a son belongs to it forever" (John 8:34–35). Servants don't wake up in the morning and give orders; masters do. Sinful pleasures give the illusion of freedom, but they are the worst kind of bondage.

At Christmas I saw a child in a stroller, frantically turning his toy steering wheel to the right while his stroller veered left. His puny steering wheel was not connected to anything that mattered. He could angrily turn it whatever direction he liked, but his mother was in charge. Just so, sin gives us the illusion of control, but the steering mechanism is, for the most part, disconnected. We obediently obey our lusts. Not we, but sin, has the last word.

One of the tragedies of the nineteenth century was the career of Oscar Wilde. Though he had a brilliant mind and won the highest rewards in literature, he fell prey to the temptations of unnatural vice and ended in prison in disgrace. He admitted:

> The gods have given me almost everything. But I let myself be lured into long spells of senseless and sensual ease. . . . Tired of being on the heights I deliberately went to the depths in search for a new sensation. What the paradox was to me in the sphere of thought, perversity became to me in the sphere of passion. . . . I took pleasure where it pleased me, and passed on. I forgot that little actions of the common day makes or unmakes character, and that therefore what one has done in the secret chamber, one has some day to cry aloud from the housetop. I was no longer the captain of my soul and did not know it. I allowed pleasure to dominate me. I ended in horrible disgrace.[14]

Desire is a bad master. The pleasures of sin are overrated; they are mislabeled. "At one time we too were foolish, disobedient, deceived and enslaved by all kinds of passions and pleasures. We lived in malice and envy, being hated and hating one another. But when the kindness and love of God our Savior appeared, he saved us, not because of righteous things we had done, but because of his mercy" (Titus 3:3–5). We are foolish when we look at the world and think we have been gypped. Ask Oscar Wilde and he will tell you that sin always takes you farther than you wanted to go, keeps you longer than you intended to stay, and costs you more than you intended to pay.

An addiction is God's way of telling us that sin is a bad idea. We can see the deception of sin most clearly in matters such as alcoholism, gambling, and sexual obsession. But the same thing happens with "the sins of the spirit," that is, greed, jealousy, and self-aggrandizement. Our problem is that these pleasures can present themselves as overwhelming. We cannot imagine life without them; we think that they are a part of who we are.

There is a story about a kite that said to itself, "If only I could get rid of that string that holds me back, I could fly as high as I wished; but the string restricts me from being free." One evening the kite got its wish. The string snapped, and at last the kite was free to fly above the clouds toward the stars. But almost instantly it came crashing to the ground because the string that holds a kite down is the string that holds it up. There is a lesson here for us: if we want to fly beyond the clouds, we must let God be in control.

## Spiritual Maturity Is Substituting the Greater Pleasures for the Lesser

How can the pleasures of God compete with the euphoria of, say, pornography? What about the pleasures of immorality or drugs or drink? Or the "high" that comes from gambling? Or the pleasures of self-promotion, self-absorption, and self-preservation? Even the pleasure that comes from retaining hatred in our hearts? How could the pleasures that God holds out to us be as satisfying as these?

God satisfies us in a way that other pleasures cannot. He gives us that which is of highest value; He gives us Himself. To quote Pascal again:

There once was in man a true happiness of which now remains to him only the mark of an empty trace, which he in vain tries to fill from all his surroundings, seeking from things absent the help he does not obtain in things present. But these are all inadequate, because the infinite abyss can only be filled by an infinite and immutable object, that is to say, only God Himself.[15]

C. S. Lewis wrote that in the Psalms God is the "all-satisfying Object." His people rejoice in Him for the "exceeding joy" they have in Him. "Though you have not seen him, you love him; and even though you do not see him now, you believe in him and are filled with an *inexpressible and glorious joy,* for you are receiving the goal of your faith, the salvation of your souls" (1 Pet. 1:8–9, emphasis mine).

David also spoke of this joy:

> LORD, you have assigned me my portion and my cup;
>> you have made my lot secure.
> The boundary lines have fallen for me in pleasant places;
>> surely I have a delightful inheritance.
> I will praise the LORD, who counsels me;
>> even at night my heart instructs me.
> I have set the LORD always before me.
>> Because he is at my right hand,
>> I will not be shaken.
> Therefore my heart is glad and my tongue rejoices;
>> my body also will rest secure,
> because you will not abandon me to the grave,
>> nor will you let your Holy One see decay.
> You have made known to me the path of life;
>> you will fill me with joy in your presence,
>> with eternal pleasures at your right hand.
>
> (Ps. 16:5–11)

In the early verses of this psalm, David turns away from false gods. He realizes the bankruptcy of false loves that cannot keep their promises.

He turns from the impure pleasures that always leave an aftertaste and whose reward is an empty soul.

He looks around and sees that God has surrounded him with blessings. He thinks back to the time when the Israelites entered the land and it was divided up according to the casting of lots. He realizes that his lot in life has been very good: "The boundary lines have fallen for me in pleasant places; surely I have a delightful inheritance" (v. 6). Today we must take a moment to remember the goodness of God in our own lives. Those of us who have come to faith in Christ have an indescribable inheritance that we cannot take for granted.

As David looks to the challenges ahead, he honors the Lord in his mind and heart. "I have set the LORD always before me. Because he is at my right hand, I will not be shaken" (v. 8). David gives the Lord the position of honor and dignity. Someone has said that David "buries himself, beelike, in the pure delights of communion with the Lord." Years earlier, when David repented of his backsliding, he wrote, "Taste and see that the LORD is good; blessed is the man who takes refuge in him" (Ps. 34:8). There is no pleasure like that of savoring a relationship with God.

This acknowledgment of God's blessings has two benefits. First, there is a present sense of fulfillment: "Therefore my heart is glad and my tongue rejoices" (v. 9). David has found the happiness that we all so naturally seek. Imagine rejoicing without guilt, without regrets, and with true freedom. Of course I do not mean that David never had a bad day (in fact, if you read the Psalms you know that he almost always had a bad day). But he knew that he would rather have a bad day with God than have a good day with just himself and his own pleasures. It is not contradictory to say that there is joy in the midst of sorrow and happiness in the midst of pain.

Second, there is a future benefit. His body, he says, will rest secure "because you will not abandon me to the grave, nor will you let your Holy One see decay" (v. 10). He will descend to the grave in hope of a future life; he will die with confidence, and even in death he will find joy: "You have made known to me the path of life; you will fill me with joy in your presence, with eternal pleasures at your right hand" (v. 11).

Let's not miss the fact that in this life the Lord is at David's right hand, and in the life to come David will be at the Lord's right hand! As we now honor God, so we shall some day be honored. And the joy will be pure, exuberant, and eternal.

Could we feel otherwise in the presence of God, beholding His beauty and knowing His acceptance? Surely such joy will be our experience in the life to come, but even now we have a taste of the divine blessing.

## God's Pleasures and Our Pleasures Are in Harmony

Getting to know God does not mean the renunciation of joy but rather the fulfillment of it. We worship that which we adore, that in which we delight. What if God sends us to the mission field? What if a member of our family dies? What if all of our emotional needs are not met? The scriptural answer is that it is better to travel a difficult road with the blessing of God than to blaze our own trail without the intimacy of His fellowship. What is best for God is best for us; whatever brings God pleasure is most rewarding for us. Pursue the wrong pleasures and you get nothing; pursue God and you get it all. As C. S. Lewis said, you have satisfaction in this life and "heaven thrown in." Jerry Walls was right: "In our age, as in every age, people are longing for happiness, not realizing that what they are looking for is holiness."[16]

What most glorifies God is also best for us.

## A PERSONAL RESPONSE

George Mueller (1805–98) was a great man of prayer and faith. He established orphanages in England not just to take care of needy children but also to demonstrate God's trustworthiness. He never asked for funds but relied on prayer alone; his life is a history of miracles. He learned something that revolutionized his relationship with God: "I saw more clearly than ever, that the first great and primary business to which I ought to attend every day was, to have my soul happy in God. The first thing to be concerned about was not how much I might serve the Lord, how I might glorify the Lord; but how I might get my soul into a happy state, and how my inner man might be nourished."[17]

He goes on to say that he gave himself to the reading of the New Testament every morning. There he practiced confession and petition mingled with meditation until his heart was at rest in the presence of the Almighty. Only then did he begin his day with his soul nourished.

Let us learn from his example. If you are not presently beginning your day in the presence of God, let me urge you to do so. No matter how much effort it costs us, we will be rewarded with the assurance that there is genuine joy in the presence of God. Twenty minutes a day will change our lives. Read one psalm a day and one chapter from the New Testament. "He who has God and everything else," the Puritans used to say, "does not have more than he who has God only." Fanny Crosby wrote:

O, the pure delight of a single hour that before the throne I spend,
When I kneel in prayer, and with thee my God
I commune as friend with friend!
Draw me nearer, nearer blessed Lord
To the cross where thou hast died
Draw me nearer, nearer, nearer blessed Lord
To thy precious bleeding side.

*(Draw Me Nearer)*

Let us make our delight in God our first priority.

# LIE 10

# God Helps Those
# Who Help Themselves

THERE IS A STORY ABOUT A MAN who was stranded in his house during a flood. A boat came to rescue him while he was standing on his doorstep, surrounded by water. But he waived the rescuer off, saying, "God will rescue me!" The following day the water rose and another boat came to rescue the man now stuck on the upstairs balcony. He again refused help, shouting, "God will rescue me!" Late the next day, he found himself sitting on the chimney, the waters swirling around him. A helicopter hovered overhead, a man shouting, "Let us help you!" But he shouted back, "God will rescue me!"

As fate would have it, the water rose and the man drowned. He arrived in heaven in a not-so-good mood, complaining to Saint Peter, "I expected you to rescue me!"

"Frankly, I'm surprised to see you here," Peter replied, "because we sent two boats and a helicopter to pick you up!" We can almost hear Peter say, "Remember, *God helps those who help themselves.*"

According to the George Barna Research Associates, eight out of ten Americans believe that the statement "God helps those who help themselves" is found in the Bible.[1] It seems evident that we have to do our part if we expect God to do His. Why should we count on God to do everything? Only if we do what we can should we expect His help to do what we cannot.

This reasonable principle is based on two assumptions. The first is the need and value of work. We resent giving to those who are lazy; if a person chooses to help himself, we will help him, but he also must put forth effort. We expect our children to do some work: we say, "I will pay for college if you get a job during the summer and earn at least enough for your extra expenses. I will help you if you help yourself first because you have to become worthy of my involvement, of my sacrifice. Why should you receive something for nothing?" We despise laziness.

Second, this slogan is based on the assumption of ability, that is, that there is actually something you can do; you can take the first step. If you had a disability that made work impossible, then of course we would not expect you to "help yourself." But if you are well and capable, we will help you if you put forth some effort. We will meet you halfway; in fact, we might meet you more than halfway; but please understand that you can't expect us to do it all. There is no free lunch; somebody has to pay, and it might as well be you.

Our temptation is to assume that God thinks like we do about such matters. But God is not a man. We have already learned that we make a mistake when we too quickly attribute human characteristics to Him. We must test our understanding of God with Scripture; we must try to understand what He has said about Himself before we attribute our attitudes to Him.

In one way, there is some truth to the statement "God helps those who help themselves." The Bible warns about taking advantage of God's blessings without acknowledging our obligation to serve Him to the best of our ability. For example, Paul said that if a man didn't work, he shouldn't eat (2 Thess. 3:10). We can't lounge around, thinking God should do everything for us. He does expect us to take advantage of a boat or a helicopter if we need to be rescued. There are some things we can do first and then God will help us. James tells believers, "Come near to God and he will come near to you" (James 4:8).

But—and this is important—for every time "God helps those who help themselves," there are a dozen instances in which God helps those who *cannot* help themselves. In fact, if He didn't help those who cannot help themselves, we would all be lost. As we shall see in a moment, only those who know that they cannot help themselves receive the grace of forgiveness; indeed, our salvation turns on the recognition that we absolutely can do nothing to help ourselves; God even has to grant us the ability to receive the free gift!

For the record, the statement "God helps those who help themselves" is not in the Bible; it originated in pagan religion. Five hundred years before Christ, Aesop wrote, "The gods help them that help themselves." Euripides, a Greek philosopher, said, "Try first thyself, and after, call on God." And George Herbert of the seventeenth century said, "Help thyself and God will help thee." We received our present formulation from Benjamin Franklin: "God helps those who help themselves."

This statement is an enemy of grace, and if Franklin believed it, it contributed to his rejection of the gospel. As a deist, Franklin was a firm believer in God and divine providence, but he could not accept the deity of Christ. He was a close friend of the great evangelist George Whitefield, who pleaded with people to repent and believe the gospel. But despite a warm and mutually helpful friendship lasting thirty years, Franklin wrote after his friend died, "Whitefield used to pray for my conversion, but never had the satisfaction of believing that his prayers were heard."[2] And as death approached, Franklin saw no reason to believe, since he said he would shortly know whether it was true or not.

Whether we can help ourselves depends on what our problem is. If our most pressing problem is ignorance, we can help ourselves by getting an education; if it is the need to express our deepest feelings, we can get help from a psychiatrist. If we are drowning, we just might be able to struggle to safety, or a lifeguard might be able to rescue us. Unfortunately, our problem is far greater than all of these. If you are dead, you have a God-sized problem. Resurrection is something only God can do.

When it comes to our redemption, God must intervene to save us because we cannot help ourselves. In fact, as long as we think we can help ourselves, we will never be rescued. Understanding both the extent of our need and the extent of God's power lies at the heart of the gospel message. Stay with me as I explain.

## OUR DILEMMA BEFORE CONVERSION

Read these lines and ask yourself if there is anything we can do to save ourselves: "As for you, you were dead in your transgressions and sins, in which you used to live when you followed the ways of this world and of the ruler of the kingdom of the air, the spirit who is now at work in those who are disobedient" (Eph. 2:1–2).

Before we were converted, we were *dead* in transgressions and sins. We do not stop en route to a cemetery to buy medicine for our friends buried there. If they were sick, a right dosage of prescription drugs might help, but they are beyond medicine. Just so, spiritually speaking, without Christ we are dead, not just sick; we are cut off from God and incapable of connecting with Him.

I have a friend who has a photograph of the corpse of the philosopher Jeremy Bentham. Bentham's body is propped up in a chair, dressed and hatted in early nineteenth-century gentleman's wear. When he was alive, Bentham gave orders that his entire estate be given to the University College Hospital in London on the condition that his body be preserved and placed at attendance at all the hospital's board meetings. This, so far as I know, is still duly carried out to this day. His corpse is wheeled up to the board table and the chairman says, "Jeremy Bentham, present, but not voting." Since his death in 1832, he has not voted on any motion, nor has he submitted any legislation!

*Present, but not voting!* That's what we are, spiritually speaking, without the intervention of Christ. Those who are dead might be very alive physically; they can go to an opera, earn money, and ski in Colorado. Yes, we can do all those things and a whole lot more besides; but spiritually, without Christ we are dead, that is, disconnected from God.

Have you had the experience of talking to someone who does not want to hear what you have to say? He filters and reinterprets every statement; your words do not connect with his heart. That is perhaps a better way to picture us before God's grace intervened in our lives. "Even from birth the wicked go astray; from the womb they are wayward and speak lies. Their venom is like the venom of a snake, like that of a cobra that has stopped its ears, that will not heed the tune of the charmer, however skillful the enchanter may be" (Ps. 58:3–5). That's not a flattering picture, but when we get a better grasp on who we are at the core of our being, we will agree that the description is not overblown.

Apart from God's intervention, we are also blind. Left to ourselves, spiritually speaking, we neither see our need nor grasp the wonder of the gospel. "The god of this age has blinded the minds of unbelievers, so that they cannot see the light of the gospel of the glory of Christ, who is the image of God" (2 Cor. 4:4). I hope you are beginning to understand why we are not able to "help ourselves." Of course we compound our problem by telling ourselves that we are alive and can hear and can see. "But the way of the wicked is like deep darkness; they do not know what makes them stumble" (Prov. 4:19).

Our inner desires mislead us, but so does an outer enemy. Paul says we follow "the spirit who is now at work in those who are disobedient. All of us also lived among them at one time, gratifying the cravings of our sinful nature and following its desires and thoughts. Like the rest, we were by nature objects of wrath" (Eph. 2:2–3). Satan puts thoughts into our minds that we think are our own; this adds to our desire to be deceived. If we were just sick, we might find a cure; if we just had glaucoma, a surgeon might help us. But we are dead, and we are blind; no wonder we are deceived.

Some people think our problem is our environment; change circumstances and that in turn will change us. Others think that our need is lack of self-esteem, so our great hope is psychiatry. Yes, our environment is important and counselors can help us, but neither can connect us with God. They can't give us divine life; they cannot bring us up from our spiritual and moral graveyards.

## GOD'S POWER TO SAVE US

Thankfully, God comes to visit the cemetery.

> But because of his great love for us, God, who is rich in mercy, made us alive with Christ even when we were dead in transgressions—it is by grace you have been saved. And God raised us up with Christ and seated us with him in the heavenly realms in Christ Jesus, in order that in the coming ages he might show the incomparable riches of his grace, expressed in his kindness to us in Christ Jesus.
>
> (Eph. 2:4–7)

When did God intervene? *While we were dead.* He came to us at a time when we could not help ourselves. We could make no contribution to what He chose to do. Resurrections are the work of an omnipotent God. When Jesus was at the tomb of Lazarus, He did not say, "Now, Lazarus, I will help you if you just help yourself a little bit. I will not require much; I will do more than My share, but you must at least wiggle your toes. If you do that much, I will take over from there."

Every fall semester, I teach a course in preaching at Trinity International University. Again this year, I asked my students to meet me at a cemetery, where I urged them to preach to the dead. Before me was the tombstone of a couple who died in 1912. I asked one of the students to preach, to tell them it was resurrection morning! So far, every year, every student has refused, not believing that I could be serious.

So I went over to the grave and shouted that the dead were to "come forth." Then I waited for a response. When there was no response (thankfully!), I had some fun with the students, telling them that the dead did not arise only because they were unable to hear; if I shouted loudly enough, they would respond! So I shouted instructions to arise because it was resurrection morning. Again I waited, and quite predictably, there was no response.

Then I turned to the students and asked, "How do you think I felt doing this?" They answered correctly: "Very foolish!" But that is how foolish we are every time we preach the good news of the gospel; we are commanding the dead to arise, the deaf to hear, and the blind to see! And yet we are not foolish, for God just might raise the dead and open the ears of the deaf and cause the eyes of the blind to see. As Paul put it, "For since in the wisdom of God the world through its wisdom did not know him, God was pleased through the foolishness of what was preached to save those who believe" (1 Cor. 1:21).

When God saves us, He activates His resurrection power. He creates something within us that was not there before. "Therefore, if anyone is in Christ, he is a new creation; the old has gone, the new has come!" (2 Cor. 5:17). God must invade our private world; He is the One who must come to us. He cannot wait for us to "do the best we can."

Let me give you some encouragement. Obviously it is not more difficult to raise someone who has been dead for ten years than someone who has been dead for three days. The condition of the corpse makes no difference in the presence of an omnipotent God. Just so, it is not more difficult for God to save "big" sinners than to save "lesser" ones. Dead is dead, and a resurrection is a resurrection. You might think that your sin is too great, your past too sordid. But there is more grace in God's heart than there is sin in your past. The issue is not the greatness of our sin but the application of God's powerful remedy.

## GOD'S PURPOSE IN SAVING US

What is God's purpose in performing these "resurrections"? Paul gives two in the passage from Ephesians. "And God raised us up with Christ and seated us with him in the heavenly realms in Christ Jesus, in order that in the coming ages he might show the incomparable riches of his grace, expressed in his kindness to us in Christ Jesus" (Eph. 2:6–7). The first reason God came to save us is to display His grace; God wants to put us on exhibit so that in the coming ages His undeserved mercy will be evident to all: to angels, to demons, to men, and anyone else who might catch a glimmer of God's generosity. The first purpose of the cross is always God-directed. For example, Paul says that God set forth Christ "to demonstrate his justice" (Rom. 3:25).

When the Reverend Paul Gibson retired as principal of Cambridge, in honor of his service, a portrait of him was commissioned and unveiled. In expressing thanks, Gibson paid a well-deserved compliment to the artist, saying that in the future people looking at the picture would not ask, "Who is that man?" but rather, "Who painted the portrait?"[3] Just so, throughout eternity people will not ask, "Who are the redeemed?" but rather, "Who is the Redeemer?" Who could possibly take such sinners and elevate them to a position of prominence and honor? Who could take those who are least deserving and raise them up with Christ, that they might be seated with Him at the Father's right hand?

The second purpose of God's salvation is directed toward us. In these verses three words describe God's benevolence for sinners. Let's read it again, emphasizing those words: "Because of his great *love* for us, God, who is rich in *mercy*, made us alive with Christ even when we were dead in transgressions—it is by *grace* you have been saved" (Eph. 2:4–5, emphasis mine). Grace is giving us what we don't deserve; mercy is shielding us from what we do deserve. When God rescued us, He got what He wanted, namely, glory; we get what we want, namely, His kindness.

Think this through: When God raised Christ up, that was an act of power. When He raised us up, it was an act of power, but also of mercy. Christ deserved to be raised; we did not. Mozart in his requiem has a wonderful line, "Help me to remember that I was the cause of Your journey."

Does God "help those who help themselves"? As humans we might think that we have to help God, that we must do something before we are blessed. But Paul set the record straight: "Now when a man works, his wages are not credited to him as a gift, but as an obligation. However, to the man who does not work but trusts God who justifies the wicked, his faith is credited as righteousness" (Rom. 4:4–5). Far from helping those who help themselves, God helps only those who *cannot help themselves*. God is attracted not to our strength, but to our weakness; not to how capable we are, but to how incapable we are. He is the God of resurrection.

Keep in mind that good works follow our conversion. Immediately after Paul pointedly taught that we are saved by grace through faith, he added, "For we are God's workmanship, created in Christ Jesus to do good works, which God prepared in advance for us to do" (Eph. 2:10). Before our conversion God helps only those of us who know we cannot help ourselves; after our conversion He helps us so that we can "help ourselves." After we are raised from the dead, we become "God's fellow workers" (1 Cor. 3:9).

Explain this good news called the gospel to someone and he might respond, "If salvation is a free gift, then after I receive it, it is mine forever. So I can accept it and live like I please, committing any sin or crime, and still go to heaven." Such a response does not take into account the radical change that God's intervention brings to the human heart. When we are "born again" we receive a new nature, with new affections and a love for God. Good works after saving faith help confirm that our conversion is genuine.

## THE DIFFICULTY OF ACCEPTING GRACE

God's grace is difficult to accept for two different kinds of people; first, those who are awash with guilt: drug addicts, alcoholics, prostitutes, and the like. They think, *God is so mad at me that there is no way that He would accept me*. When we explain God's grace to them, they feel too unworthy to accept it.

A second class of people who find it difficult to accept grace are the self-righteous people who do volunteer work, who have never been in trouble with the law, who pay their bills and keep their noses in their own business. The hardworking folks who are basically honest, who can look around and see a dozen people who are worse off than they are, find God's grace offensive. The very notion that they cannot contribute to their own redemption is an insult to their sense of accomplishment and well-being. This is why Jesus said to the religious types of His day, "I tell you the truth, the tax collectors and the prostitutes are entering the kingdom of God ahead of you" (Matt. 21:31). Pity those who don't accept God's grace because they are "helping themselves" and therefore wrongly think that they will do fine in the day of judgment. Jesus has nothing to give to those who have no need.

A friend of mine grew up in a home where he was told, "God helps those who help themselves." As a teenager he began with petty theft, then graduated to the more risky life of a car thief. Drugs and alcohol consumed him; more thievery became necessary to support his habits. The thought that "God helps those who help themselves" drove him to despair. Where and how would he begin helping himself? He broke resolutions to change almost as quickly as he made them; suicide seemed like an attractive alternative to his addictions. Not until he learned that God helps those who *cannot* help themselves was he converted and set free from his sinful lifestyle.

God always takes the first step. He comes to us when we finally have given up on our own attempts to save ourselves. As David Hubbard expressed it, "In a massive conspiracy of grace, the Father, Son and Holy Spirit plotted together to turn our lives around."[4] Our contribution is to do what Lazarus did: respond when God calls us.

Simon Wiesenthal, who himself lived through the Holocaust and does not want us to forget that wretched part of human history, wrote a book titled *The Sunflower*. In it he grapples with the subject of guilt, relating that one day he was brought from a death camp to a makeshift army hospital. There he was ushered to the side of a dying Nazi soldier who had asked to have a few private moments with a Jew. Wiesenthal entered the room hesitantly, not knowing what to expect. He was brought face to face with a fatally wounded man, bandaged from head to toe. The suffering soldier turned to him and spoke in a whisper, unburdening his heart of the heinous crime he had committed when he set a village of Jews ablaze. His mind constantly replayed the screams of those women and children as they burned to death. His conscience knew no peace. Knowing that he was dying, he was making a desperate effort to seek forgiveness from one whose people he had killed.

Wiesenthal could not bring himself to grant the dying man's request. In fact, he made numerous attempts to leave, but the suffering solider implored him to stay. The soldier needed to get this atrocity off his heart; he needed to receive forgiveness. But Wiesenthal thought it impossible that, with a wave of the hand, he could absolve so terrible a crime against humanity. And who was he to think that he could offer forgiveness for the dead, whose cries the young man heard in his own tormented mind?

Later Wiesenthal pondered whether he had done the right thing. Perhaps he should have granted the soldier his dying wish. So he wrote to thirty-two men and women of high regard and asked them their opinion. Twenty-six agreed with Wiesenthal's decision: he should not have thought he could forgive a crime against a whole race; he could not speak for the dead. Six suggested that he should have taken the high road, and at least speaking for himself, grant the dying man the pardon he sought.

Ravi Zacharias has pointed out that Wiesenthal's predicament was genuine, but so was the plight of the Nazi soldier who sought forgiveness in the last hour of his life. Certainly Wiesenthal could not have spoken for the dead; what is more, he could not have spoken on behalf of God whose forgiveness the Nazi really needed.[5] My point lies in a different direction: imagine standing at the bedside of this dying man and saying, "Remember, God helps those who help themselves."

We have not committed the crimes of this solider, but we do have this in common: we cannot help ourselves by doing good works that we hope will reconcile us to God. Simply put, we lack the goodness God demands. Thus, despite obvious differences in lifestyle between us, we as well as the Nazi stand condemned at the bar of God's holiness. And if this soldier had believed in Christ, he, too, would have entered into heaven, for God gives the same gift of righteousness to all who believe and performs the same miracle in their hearts.

In the movie *The Last Emperor,* the young child anointed as leader of China lives a magical life of luxury with a thousand eunuch servants at his command. "What happens when you do wrong?" his brother asks. "When I do wrong, someone else is punished," the young emperor replies. To demonstrate, he breaks a jar and one of the servants is beaten.

In Christian theology, Christ does one better than that. In the movie, the emperor does wrong and a servant is beaten; in Christianity, the servants do wrong and the Emperor is beaten. In the presence of God, we are always in the wrong, but thankfully, Christ puts us in the right. That is grace.

I speak today to those who cannot help themselves; the more crippled you are by your sin, the better your chances of seeing your need. I invite you to come to "the God of all grace" who is able to build you up in the most holy faith. And when we come, our lives are transformed.

> For the grace of God that brings salvation has appeared to all men. It teaches us to say "No" to ungodliness and worldly passions, and to live self-controlled, upright and godly lives in this present age, while we wait for the blessed hope—the glorious appearing of our great God and Savior, Jesus Christ, who gave himself for us to redeem us from all wickedness and to purify for himself a people that are his very own, eager to do what is good.
>
> (Titus 2:11–14)

## A PERSONAL RESPONSE

Your response to this chapter depends on where you are in your spiritual journey. Those of us who have transferred our trust to Christ can take a few moments to worship God, thanking Him for rescuing us from our own waywardness. We can contemplate the promise that "in the coming ages" we will show "the incomparable riches of his grace."

For you who have, possibly for the first time, grasped your need for God's personal intervention in your life, it is time to simply admit that you cannot help yourself. As emphasized, God will not redeem you until you lose all confidence in your own goodness and transfer your faith to Christ alone.

Jesus told a story about two men who went into a temple to pray. The first stood praising God that he was such a good man. "God, I thank you that I am not like other men—robbers, evildoers, adulterers—or even like this tax collector. I fast twice a week and give a tenth of all I get" (Luke 18:11–12).

But the tax collector approached God differently. He "stood at a distance. He would not even look up to heaven, but beat his breast and said, 'God, have mercy on me, a sinner'" (v. 13). Jesus added that this man went home justified but the other did not. When it comes to grace, we bring nothing to the table except our great need. God makes up for our deficiency; He responds to those who cannot help themselves and know it. Having received it, our lives are transformed. At this moment, tell God you are making that transfer of trust.

Augustine said that grace can be received only with empty hands.

# Epilogue:
# Can We Trust Him?

WARS, POVERTY, NATURAL DISASTERS, and horrendous injustices exist on this planet. Who can possibly calculate the buckets of tears that human beings are shedding at any given hour in this fallen world? Can we trust a sovereign God who could, at any moment, put an end to such suffering yet doesn't? A God who could have prevented the catastrophes that have pounded the world throughout the centuries? A God who could have had Hitler die as an infant in his mother's arms?

There are some encounters with evil that are so horrific they challenge the foundations of faith in a benevolent God; for some, that faith is destroyed. Elie Wiesel has written for millions of Jews and other victims of the Holocaust, and we must hear his anguish:

> Never shall I forget that night, the first night in camp, which has turned my life into one long night, seven times cursed and seven times sealed. Never shall I forget that smoke. Never shall I forget the faces of the children whose bodies I saw turned into wreaths of smoke beneath a silent blue sky.
>
> Never shall I forget those flames which consumed my faith forever.[1]

Can we trust Him?

Before we answer, let us feel the pathos, the emotional agony, and the disappointment in God expressed in Wiesel's words. We can understand why the flames could consume one's faith forever. To disbelieve in God, however, is hardly comforting in the face of such wanton evil. For if God does not exist, then there is no possibility that the injustices of the past will be rectified. A Jewish friend of mine who is an atheist admitted that he felt some disquiet of spirit to know that Hitler would never be judged for what he did; he had no hope that there would be a final reckoning that would set the record straight. To not believe in God is not the answer.

On the other hand, we should not think that we have an adequate, purely rational answer to Elie Wiesel's dilemma. The difficulty of reconciling human suffering with the existence of a good and powerful God challenges our best minds. After all the theological essays have been written and the debaters have become silent, we still do not understand it; we stand in awe of great mystery. John Stackhouse has written,

> The God of predestination, the God of worldwide providence, the God who created all and sustains all and thus ultimately is responsible for all—this God has revealed to us only a glimpse of the divine cosmic plan. God has not let us see in any comprehensive way the sense in suffering, the method in the madness. God has chosen instead to remain a mystery.[2]

Yes, God has chosen to remain a mystery. In his book *On First Principles,* Origen described what Paul meant when he wrote that God's judgments are "unsearchable" (Rom. 11:33) and His ways unfathomable (Ps. 145:3). Just read these words:

> Paul did not say that God's judgments were hard to search out but that they could not be searched out at all. He did not say that God's ways were hard to find out but that they were impossible to find out. For however far one may advance in the search and make progress

through an increasing earnest study, even when aided and enlightened
in the mind by God's grace, he will never be able to reach the final goal
of his inquiries.[3]

In order to illustrate the demands of faith, the philosopher Basil
Mitchell tells this parable: In time of war in an occupied country, a
member of the resistance meets with a stranger one night who deeply
impresses him. They spend the night together in conversation. The
stranger affirms that he also is on the side of the resistance—indeed, he
is in charge of it. He urges the young partisan to have faith in him, no
matter what. The young man is impressed with the stranger and decides
to believe in him.

The next day he sees the stranger fight on the side of the resistance,
and he says to his friends, "See, the stranger is on our side." His faith is
vindicated.

But the following day the stranger is in the uniform of a policeman,
handing patriots to the occupying power—to the enemy!

The young man's friends murmur against him, insisting that the
stranger could not be on their side, because he was seen helping the enemy.
But the young partisan is undeterred, believing resolutely in the stranger.

Sometimes he asks for help from the stranger and receives it; sometimes he asks for help and does not receive it. In times of such discour-
agement he affirms, "The stranger knows best."

This ambiguous behavior on the part of the stranger causes the
young man's friends to ridicule his faith, saying, "If that's what he means
by being on our side, the sooner he goes over to the other side, the better!" Now the young man faces a dilemma: does he conclude that the
stranger is not on his side after all, or does he go on believing, no matter what?

There are two lessons in this parable. First, whether or not we will
continue to believe depends on the meeting we have had with Christ. If
in Jesus we see God close to us, loving us, forgiving us our sin, then we
will be able to go on believing even though we do not have a final answer

to the question of suffering in this life. Luther, in pondering the mystery of God's ways, urges us to "flee the hidden God and run to Christ."

Of course, the "hidden God" and the God who was made flesh are one and the same; they are not separate divinities from which we must choose. But as Stackhouse points out, it is precisely because the two are one that Luther's advice works. "One must run away from the mysteries of God's providence about which we cannot know enough to understand (because God has revealed so little about them), and run toward Jesus Christ in whom we find God adequately revealed."[4] Jesus assures us in His Word that He is for us and that nothing shall separate us from His love. Yet His actions are ambiguous; sometimes it seems as if He is not on our side at all. What do we do? At what point do we give up hope and say, "He does not care"?

The stamina of our belief depends on the extent of our friendship with the stranger (Christ). The better we know Him, the more likely we will keep trusting Him, even when His actions are confusing and He no longer seems to be on our side. We will not judge His love for us by our circumstances, but by His promises. To quote Stackhouse once more: "We can respond properly to evil in our lives because *we know that God is all-good and all-powerful because we know Jesus*" (emphasis mine).[5]

This is the trial of our faith. Jesus has come to reveal the Father to us. And through Him we know that God sees how much we are able to endure while we continue to believe that He knows best. When God chooses to do the opposite of what we think a God of love should do, that is a test of our loyalty. Suppose God wanted to create a set of circumstances that would stretch our faith in His goodness and loving concern. How could He best do that, except by making it look as if He is acting in a way that belies those exact attributes? When He appears to be on the side of the enemy, do we still believe that He knows best? Can we believe Him, no matter what?

Jesus comforts us: "Do not let your hearts be troubled. Trust in God; trust also in me. In my Father's house are many rooms; if it were not so,

I would have told you. I am going there to prepare a place for you. And if I go and prepare a place for you, I will come back and take you to be with me that you also may be where I am. You know the way to the place where I am going" (John 14:1–4).

"If He wasn't there for me before, why should I think He will be there for me now?" a woman asked me. She had been abused as a child, and as an adult she struggled with anger and distrust toward God. She could not understand how her heavenly Father, who has all power at His disposal, could possibly not intervene when she was being brutally raped and whipped. Thankfully she does believe, but it is difficult; every inch of spiritual growth is contested. Yes, ultimately our faith will be dependent on the One in whom we have come to trust.

This leads me to a second lesson from the parable: questions about the mystery of evil are not solved in this life but in the next. Recall that on some days it appeared as if the stranger was on the side of the enemy and the conflict dragged on without resolution. But remember that God has all of eternity to explain to us (if He should so desire) the mystery of His ways. As for believers, we agree with Paul, "I consider that our present sufferings are not worth comparing with the glory that will be revealed in us" (Rom. 8:18). And again: "Therefore we do not lose heart. Though outwardly we are wasting away, yet inwardly we are being renewed day by day. For our light and momentary troubles are achieving for us an eternal glory that far outweighs them all. So we fix our eyes not on what is seen, but on what is unseen. For what is seen is temporary, but what is unseen is eternal" (2 Cor. 4:16–18).

Does our heavenly Father really love us more than an earthly father who is more immediately responsive to our needs and requests? The answer is that our heavenly Father loves us more than our earthly father possibly could, but He has a different set of priorities. We value health, and so does our heavenly Father; but He values our faith even more. He delights in providing food for us, but He delights even more when we trust though we are hungry and even starving to death. And yes, He delights when we trust Him even when He does not seem to be there when we need Him.

After years of reading and thinking about the problem of reconciling the suffering of this world with the love of God, I have concluded that there might not be an acceptable rational solution. As I have tried to point out in this book, we must humbly confess that God's ways are "past finding out." He has simply not chosen to reveal all the pieces of the puzzle. But like Tony Campolo says, "It's [Good] Friday, but Sunday is coming!"

After John the Baptist was thrown into prison, he began to have second thoughts as to whether or not Christ was the Messiah. For one thing, the Old Testament predicted that when the Messiah came, He would free the prisoners (Isa. 61:1). John made the same error as those who believe God is obligated to heal us today: he misinterpreted the timing and application of some of God's promises.

As long as John sat in the dungeon, it seemed that Christ was reneging on the promises of Isaiah. And I'm sure he reflected on how unfair it was that he, who had played such a vital part in Christ's earthly ministry, should be summarily punished for taking a righteous stand against Herod's sinful marriage. So John sent a delegation to Christ to pointedly ask: "Are You the Expected One, or shall we look for someone else?" (Matt. 11:3, NASB).

In response, Jesus reminded John that miracles were occurring and then added, "Blessed is he who keeps from stumbling over Me" (v. 6, NASB). We could paraphrase, "Blessed is the person who is not upset with the way I run My business."

Blessed is the person who does not say, "I am never going to trust God because He did not keep me from injustice and abuse." Or blessed is the person who does not say, "I find the doctrine of hell so repulsive that I will not believe in the God of the Bible."

Blessed is the person who understands that we must trust God's heart when we cannot understand His hand; blessed is the person who knows that we must stand in awe in the presence of the mystery of God's purposes. Blessed is the person who goes on believing no matter what. Blessed is the person who lets God be God.

Before his death, one of America's great preachers, S. M. Lockridge, wrote a formative poem. I conclude this book with a few excerpts:

> He does not have to call for help,
> and you can't confuse Him.
> He doesn't need you and He doesn't need me.
> He stands alone in the solitude of Himself.

> He's august and He's unique.
> He's unparalleled; He's unprecedented:
> He's supreme and pre-eminent.

> . . . He's the superlative of everything good
> that you can call Him.
> I'm trying to tell you—you can trust Him!

> He can satisfy all of our needs
> and He can do it simultaneously.
> He supplies strength for the weak.
> He's available for the tempted and tried;
> He sympathizes and He sees.

> He guards and He guides.
> He heals the sick. He cleansed the lepers.
> He forgives sinners.
> He discharges debtors.
> He delivers the captives.
> He defends the feeble;
> He blesses the young.
> He regards the aged;
> He rewards the diligent.

He beautifies the meek.
I'm trying to tell you—you can trust Him!

. . . He's the Master of the mighty.
He's the Captain of the conquerors.
He's the Head of the heroes.
He's the Leader of the legislators.
He's the Overseer of the overcomers.
He's the Governor of the governors.
He's the Prince of princes.
He's the King of kings.
He's the Lord of lords.
You can trust Him!

. . . His yoke is easy,
His burden is light.
I wish I could describe Him to you!

He's indescribable because
He's incomprehensible.
He's irresistible and He's invincible.
You can't get Him off your hands.
You can't get Him out of your mind.
You can't outlive Him
and you can't live without Him.

. . . Death couldn't handle Him.
And thank God
the grave couldn't hold Him.

There was nobody before Him.
There will be nobody after Him.
He had no predecessor,

and He'll have no successor.
You can't impeach Him,
and He's not going to resign.
YOU CAN TRUST HIM![6]

"Hallelujah!" sang the multitude in heaven in John's vision on Patmos. "Salvation and glory and power belong to our God, for true and just are his judgments" (Rev. 19:1–2).

Yes, we can trust Him.

# Notes

PREFACE

1. Chris Stamper, "Religious Cafeteria and Other Cultural Buzz," *World Magazine*, 5 December 1998, 30.
2. Os Guinness in the introduction to Blaise Pascal, *The Mind on Fire* (Portland, Ore.: Multnomah Press, 1989), 28.
3. John R. Stott, *Romans: God's Great News for the World* (Downers Grove, Ill.: InterVarsity Press, 1994), 312.

CHAPTER 1

1. "Playing Possum." Words and music by Carly Simon © 1980, Universal-PolyGram International Publishing, Inc., a division of Universal Studios, Inc. (ASCAP) International copyright secured. All rights reserved. Used by permission.
2. Henry Scougal, *The Life of God in the Soul of Man* (Harrisonburg, Va.: Sprinkle Publications, 1986), 108.
3. Blaise Pascal, *The Mind On Fire*, ed. James M. Houston (Portland, Ore.: Multnomah Press, 1989), 109.
4. Saint Augustine, *Confessions* (London: Penguin Books, 1961), 21.
5. Donald W. McCullough, *The Trivialization of God* (Colorado Springs: NavPress, 1995), 13–14.
6. Ibid., 20.
7. Gloria Copeland, *God's Will Is Prosperity* (Fort Worth: KCP Publications, 1978).

8. McCullough, *The Trivialization of God*, 40.

9. Robert Schuller, *Self-Esteem: The New Reformation* (Waco: Word Books, 1982), 26–27, 127.

10. Joseph Haroutunian, *Piety versus Moralism: The Passion of New England Theology* (New York: Harper and Sons, 1932), 145.

11. Robert Wuthnow, "Small Groups Forge New Notions of Community and the Sacred," *Christian Century,* 8 December 1993, 1239–40.

12. Rosemary Radford Ruether quoted in Elizabeth Achtemeier, "Why God Is Not Mother," *Christianity Today,* 16 August 1993, 22.

13. Parker T. Williamson, "Sophia Upstages Jesus at Re-imaging Revival," *Good News,* July/August 1998, 34.

14. Paul Sherry quoted in Edward Plowman, "Read It and Weep," *World Magazine,* 5 December 1998, 24.

15. Neale Donald Walsch, *Conversations with God* (New York: G. P. Putman's Sons, 1996), 13.

16. Ibid., 8, 38, 39.

17. Betty J. Eadie and Curtis Taylor, *Embraced by the Light* (Placerville, Calif.: Gold Leaf, 1992).

18. Alan Jacobs, "The God of the Bestseller," *The Weekly Standard,* 6 December 1999, 32.

19. C. S. Lewis, *Miracles* (New York: Macmillan, 1960), 93.

20. David Crystal, ed., *The Cambridge Fact Finder* (England: Cambridge University Press, 1997), 3.

21. *The Encyclopedia Americana,* international ed., 582.

22. John Calvin, *Institutes of the Christian Religion,* ed. John T. McNeill, trans. Ford Lewis Battles (Philadelphia: Westminster Press, 1960), 37.

23. Quoted in McCullough, *The Trivialization of God*, 90.

24. James Walsh, ed., *The Cloud of Unknowing* (New York: Paulist Press, 1981), 121.

25. Ibid.

26. John Piper, *Desiring God: Meditations of a Christian Hedonist* (Portland, Ore.: Multnomah Press, 1986), 19.

CHAPTER 2

1. Marty Kaplan, "Ambushed by Spirituality," *Time,* 24 June 1996, 62.
2. Wayne Dyer, *Your Sacred Self* (New York: HarperCollins, 1995), xii.
3. Glenn Tinder, "Birth of a Troubled Conscience," *Christianity Today,* 26 April 1999, 33.
4. Quoted in Ravi Zacharias, *Can Man Live without God?* (Dallas: Word Publishing, 1994), 18–19.
5. Philip Yancey, *What's So Amazing about Grace?* (Grand Rapids: Zondervan Publishing House, 1997), 11.
6. McCullough, *The Trivialization of God,* 86.
7. Roland Bainton, *Here I Stand* (New York: New American Library, 1950), 30.

CHAPTER 3

1. A. W. Pink quoted in J. I. Packer, *Knowing God* (Downers Grove, Ill.: InterVarsity Press, 1973), 69.
2. Packer, *Knowing God,* 72.
3. R. C. Sproul, *The Holiness of God* (Wheaton: Tyndale Publishers, 1985), 63.
4. C. S. Lewis, *The Lion, the Witch, and the Wardrobe* (New York: Macmillan, 1950), 75–76.
5. McCullough, *The Trivialization of God,* 20.

CHAPTER 4

1. C. S. Lewis quoted in Charles Ohlrich, *The Suffering of God* (Downers Grove, Ill.: InterVarsity Press, 1982), 20.
2. Charles Cranfield quoted in John Stott, *The Cross of Christ* (Downers Grove, Ill.: InterVarsity Press, 1986), 134.

3. John Calvin quoted in Ibid., 141.

4. Ibid., 160.

5. Ibid., 151.

6. Archibald Hodge, *Commentary on the Confession of Faith* (Philadephia: Presbyterian Board of Publication, 1869), 70.

7. Dennis Ngien, "The God Who Suffers," *Christianity Today*, 3 February 1997, 40.

8. George Butterick quoted in Stott, *The Cross of Christ*, 158.

9. Steven Neill quoted in Ibid., 153.

10. P. T. Forsyth quoted in Ibid.

11. Stott, *The Cross of Christ*, 156.

12. Elie Wiesel, *Night*, trans. Stella Rodway (New York: Bantam Books, 1982), 61.

13. Ravi Zacharias, *Cries of the Heart* (Nashville, Tenn.: Word Publishing, 1998), 60.

14. Edward Shillito, "Jesus of the Scars," *Areopagus Proclamation* 10, no. 7 (April 2000).

CHAPTER 5

1. Paul Galloway, "Theologians Opening Heaven's Gate a Bit Wider," *Chicago Tribune*, 28 January 1996, 1.

2. John Stott in *Authentic Christianity*, quoted in *Christianity Today*, 6 September 1999, 104.

3. Raymond Panikkar, *The Unknown Christ of Hinduism* (London: Darton, Longman and Todd, 1965), 54.

4. John Sanders, *No Other Name* (Grand Rapids: Eerdmans Publishing Co., 1992), 208.

5. W. Gary Phillips, "Evangelical Pluralism: A Singular Problem," *Bibliotheca Sacra*, April/June 1994, 11.

6. Sanders, *No Other Name*, xvii, 3, 6.

7. Phillips, "Evangelical Pluralism: A Singular Problem," 12.

8. "Clark Pinnock's Response," in *Predestination and Free Will*, eds.

David Basinger and Randall Basinger, (Downers Grove, Ill.: InterVarsity Press, 1986), 150.

9. Clark Pinnock, *A Wideness in God's Mercy: The Finality of Jesus Christ in a World of Religions* (Grand Rapids: Zondervan Publishing House, 1992), 98, 111, 158, 172–76.

10. Ibid., 141.

11. Ibid., 77.

12. Phillips, "Evangelical Pluralism: A Singular Problem," 11, 15.

13. Carl Henry, in William V. Crocket and James G. Sigountos, eds., *Through No Fault of Their Own?* (Grand Rapids: Baker Book House, 1991), 254.

14. Jonathan Edwards quoted in John Piper, *Let the Nations Be Glad* (Grand Rapids: Baker Books, 1993), 128.

15. Benjamin B. Warfield, *The Plan of Salvation* (Grand Rapids: Eerdmans Publishing Co., 1977), 74.

CHAPTER 6

1. *Chicago Sun Times,* 5 May 1999, 1.

2. Ibid.

3. "The Lost and Helpless Flee from Hell to the Hills," *Independent Foreign News,* 26 August 1999.

4. C. H. Spurgeon, *The Treasury of the Bible, The Old Testament,* vol. 4 (Grand Rapids: Zondervan Publishing House, 1962), 212.

5. C. H. Spurgeon, *The Metropolitan Tabernacle Pulpit,* vol. 15 (Pasadena, Tex.: Pilgrim Publications, 1970), 460.

6. Albert Camus, *The Plague,* trans. Stuart Gilbert (New York: Penguin Books, 1966).

7. Hodge, *A Commentary on the Confession of Faith,* 134.

8. Timothy Lull, ed., *Martin Luther's Basic Theological Writings* (Minneapolis: Fortress Press, 1989), 744.

9. Ibid., 742.

10. John Stuart Mill, *Nature: The Utility of Religion and Theism* (Watts & Co., The Rationalist Press, 1904), 21.

11. John Piper, *World Magazine*, 4 September 1999, 33.

12. William Cowper, *Cowper's Poems*, ed. Hugh I'Anson (New York: Everyman's Library, 1966), 188–89.

13. Quoted in Charles Swindoll, *The Mystery of God's Will* (Nashville, Tenn.: Word Publishing, 1999), 115.

14. Moody Adams, *The Titanic's Last Hero* (West Colombia, S.C.: Olive Press, 1997), 23.

CHAPTER 7

1. William James quoted in Robert Morey, *Battle of the Gods* (Southbridge, Mass.: Crown Publications, 1989), 77.

2. Basinger and Basinger, eds., *Predestination and Free Will*, 97–98.

3. Gregory Boyd, *Letters from a Skeptic* (Wheaton: Victor Books, 1994), 30.

4. Richard Rice, *The Openness of God* (Nashville, Tenn.: Review and Herald, 1979), 36–37.

5. Basinger and Basinger, eds., *Predestination and Free Will*, 96.

6. John Piper, "Why the Glory of God Is at Stake in the 'Foreknowledge' Debate," *Modern Reformation*, September/October 1999, 43.

7. Ibid., 42.

8. Greg Boyd, *God at War: The Bible and Spiritual Conflict* (Downers Grove, Ill.: InterVarsity Press, 1997), 58.

9. Greg Boyd quoted in Rebecca J. Ritzel, "Marketing Heresy?" *World Magazine*, 20 November 1999, 27.

10. J. I. Packer, *Knowing God* (Downers Grove, Ill.: InterVarsity Press, 1973), 37.

CHAPTER 8

1. John Piper, *The Pleasures of God* (Portland, Ore.: Multnomah Press, 1991), 38.

2. Charles D. Alexander, *Hallelujah! For the Lord God Omnipotent Reigneth!* (Pensacola, Fla: Mt. Zion Publications), 12. From a message given at the annual meeting of the Sovereign Grace Union, London, July 1969.

3. Ibid., 16.

4. Erwin Lutzer, *Doctrines That Divide* (Grand Rapids: Kregel, 1998), 153–223. Many people think that the problem of evil can be solved by an appeal to the free will of God's creatures. This view is wholly unsatisfactory for many different reasons. First, if God planned that His creatures not sin, but He could not fulfill His plan because of their free will, we must point out that He could have chosen to create only those angels/men He foreknew would not sin, or He could have created creatures like those in heaven, always desiring to serve God and free from the ability to sin. Furthermore, it is hard to believe that free will would have been worth the horrendous suffering in this world and for many, the existence of hell in the next. Finally, if free will was so critical to God's program, one would expect that it would be taught in the Scriptures, but it is not. The Bible does not teach that we are robots, but responsible people, yet it also points out that we are not as free as those who appeal to the free will defense make us out to be. Reading these passages will dispense with the notion that God limited Himself by the free will of His creatures: Exod. 4:21; 12:36; Ps. 105:25; Prov. 21:1; Dan. 4:25; Amos 3:6; John 1:13; 5:21; 12:39–40; Acts 4:27–28; 13:48; Rom. 9:22–24; Eph. 1:4–5; 2 Thess. 2:13.

5. Alexander, *Hallelujah! For the Lord God Omnipotent Reigneth!* 2.

6. Frank Mead, ed., *12,000 Religious Quotations* (Grand Rapids: Baker Book House, 1989), 179.

7. S. C. Gwynne, "An Act of God?" *Time*, 20 December 1999, 58.

8. Charles Swindoll, *The Mystery of God's Will* (Nashville, Tenn.: Word Publishing, 1999), 91.

CHAPTER 9

1. John Piper, *Desiring God* (see note 26 under chapter 1); *The Pleasures of God* (see note 1 under chapter 8).
2. Piper, *The Pleasures of God*, 23.
3. Ibid., 31.
4. Ibid., 85.
5. Ibid., 89.
6. Ibid., 108.
7. Ibid., 61.
8. Ibid., 66.
9. Blaise Pascal, *The Mind on Fire*, 66.
10. Ibid., 108.
11. C. S. Lewis, *The Weight of Glory and Other Addresses* (Grand Rapids: Eerdmans Publishing Co., 1965), 94–95.
12. John Bartlett, *Familiar Quotations,* ed. Emily Morison Beck (Boston: Little, Brown and Company, 1968), 495.
13. John Piper, *Future Grace* (Sisters, Ore.: Multnomah Press, 1995), 8.
14. Oscar Wilde, *De Profundis,* quoted in William Barclay, *The Letters of the Galatians and Ephesians* (Edinburgh: Saint Andrew's Press, 1954), 177.
15. Pascal, *The Mind on Fire*, 109.
16. Jerry L. Walls in *Good News* (May/June 1995), quoted in *Christianity Today,* 17 July 1995, 49.
17. George Mueller quoted in Piper, *Future Grace,* 127.

CHAPTER 10

1. "Born Again Christians Ignorant of Faith, Survey Also Finds Hell's Description Divides Americans," *Barna Research Outline,* 18 March 1995, 1.
2. Arnold Dallimore, *George Whitefield* (Westchester, Ill.: Crossway Books, 1980), 453.
3. John R. W. Stott, *God's New Society: The Message of Ephesians* (Downers Grove, Ill.: InterVarsity Press, 1979), 82.

4. David Hubbard quoted in McCullough, *The Trivialization of God,* 97.

5. Zacharias, *Cries of the Heart,* 116.


EPILOGUE

1. Elie Wiesel quoted in John Stackhouse, *Can God Be Trusted? Faith and the Challenge of Evil* (New York: Oxford University Press, 1998), 47.

2. Stackhouse, *Can God Be Trusted?* 103.

3. Origen, *On First Principles* (New York: Harper and Row, 1966).

4. Stackhouse, *Can God Be Trusted?* 103.

5. Ibid., 104.

6. S. M. Lockridge, "You Can Trust Him," *Reformation and Revival,* January/February 2000, 19.

# Ten Lies about God
## Study Guide

---

### LIE 1:

### GOD IS WHATEVER WE WANT HIM TO BE

*Investigating the Lies*

A. "We are born to seek for meaning, and behind that search is our search for God."

　　1. In what ways do people you know "seek for meaning"?

　　2. How have you searched for God?

B. "The word *God* has become a canvas on which each is free to paint his own portrait of the divine; like the boy scribbling at his desk, we can draw God according to whatever specifications we please."

　　1. Describe some of the "portraits of God" you have encountered. In what kind of God (if any) do your friends and acquaintances believe?

C. "Idolatry is not just dancing around a statue of silver or gold; it is constructing a mental idea of a deity that bears little resemblance to the God who actually exists."

1. Define *idolatry* using your own terms.

2. Are you ever tempted toward this kind of idolatry? Explain.

D.  There are two main reasons why we entertain so many idolatrous ideas of God today:
    *   We are impatient with His silence in this confused age.
    *   We want a God who is more tolerant of us, less demanding, less "judgmental."
        1. In what ways do people grow impatient with God's silence? Give a few examples from your own experience.

        2. Why do people see God as intolerant, demanding, and judgmental? How would you respond to their characterizations?

E.  Consider several idols popular in our world:
    *   The God of my health and wealth
    *   The God of my emotional need
    *   The God of my gender
    *   The God of my personal self-authentication
    *   The God of my near-death experience
        1. In your own words, describe each of these modern-day idols.

        2. Which of these idols could tempt you the most easily? Why? How can you overcome this temptation?

F.  "With the loss of the biblical God has come the loss of sin; with the loss of sin comes the loss of a yardstick for behavior. With this loss comes the breakdown of society."
    1. Do you agree with this assessment? Explain.

2. Name at least one example of how society around you has broken down due to the loss of the biblical God.

G. "Only a God who judges us can save us. *Idols do not judge us, but neither can they redeem us.*"
   1. Why can't we be saved by a God who refuses to judge us?

   2. Why can't idols redeem us?

*Discovering the Truth*

A. Read Psalms 42:1; 63:1.
   1. How do these verses convey a proper frame of mind for seeking God?

   2. What advice do these verses give for someone who wants to know God?

B. Read Psalm 115:3–8.
   1. What do you learn about the biblical God in verse 3?

   2. How does the biblical God differ from idols?

   3. In what way do idol worshipers become like their idols (v. 8)?

C. Read Ezekiel 14:2–3.
   1. Where did the men described in these verses set up their idols? What is significant about this?

   2. In what way do idols become "stumbling blocks"?

   3. How does God react to this kind of idolatry (v. 3)?

D. Read Isaiah 45:15–17.
   1. How does God "hide" from us? Why do you think He does this?

   2. When God hides, the human temptation is to create a visible idol. But what is the destiny of those who worship idols (v. 16)?

   3. What is the destiny of those who worship the unseen (but real) God (v. 17)?

E. Read Isaiah 57:15.
   1. How does this verse describe God?

   2. Where does God dwell, according to this verse?

   3. Why does God dwell with the "lowly"? Are you among these "lowly"? Explain.

F. Read James 4:7–10.
   1. What does it mean to "submit" to God?

   2. What happens when we "come near to God" (v. 8)? How does one come near to God?

   3. What actions does James urge upon his readers? Why these specific actions?

   4. How does verse 10 summarize verses 7–9? How do you obey this verse? What does this verse promise to those who do obey? What does this involve?

## LIE 2:
### MANY PATHS LEAD INTO GOD'S PRESENCE

*Investigating the Lies*

A. "In the last decade sin has been defined out of existence, but if one sin still exists, it is thinking someone else is wrong."

1. In what way has sin "been defined out of existence"?

2. Why does this culture believe the only sin is to think someone else is wrong? What is flawed with this kind of "tolerance"?

B. "God is defined as an equal-opportunity employer, the universal source of energy, waiting to be tapped by all of us. What we believe is not important; the challenge is to understand ourselves in light of this higher power that is already within us."

1. In what way do some people define God as "an equal-opportunity employer, the universal source of energy"?

2. Why do some people insist it doesn't matter what we believe? How would you answer them?

C. "The good news is that the issue is not the greatness of our sin, but rather the value of God's prescribed approach. We are invited to come into the 'Most Holy Place,' but we cannot come alone."

1. What is "God's prescribed approach"?

2. Why can't we come into God's presence on our own merit?

D. "You've heard someone say, 'I have not left Christianity, but just moved beyond it into spirituality.' But strictly speaking, if you move 'beyond' Christianity, you must abandon it. Whenever you try to add to it, you subtract from it. Those who surrender the uniqueness of Christ do not simply abandon a part of the gospel message; they abandon the whole of it."

1. Why is it impossible to move "beyond" Christianity without abandoning it?

2. Why does someone surrender the whole of the gospel message when he or she surrenders the uniqueness of Christ?

E.  God will not accept four common sacrifices:
   • The gift of sincerity; some think God should receive them because they mean well.
   • The gift of service; some remember all the good they have done and think God owes them acceptance for their basic decency.
   • Some bring the gift of their own spiritual quest.
   • Many bring the gift of guilt; they flagellate themselves, believing that if they feel sorry enough, they will pay for their own sins and God will accept them.
      1. How is each of these "sacrifices" flawed as a way to gain access to God?

      2. Which of these "sacrifices" do you think is the most common? Why?

      3. Which of these "sacrifices" could most readily tempt you? Explain.

F.  "A sacrifice must be equal to the offense committed. Because our sin is against an infinite God, we need a sacrifice of infinite value. It follows that only God can supply the sacrifice that He Himself demands. That is the meaning of the gospel: God met His own requirements for us."

1. Why must a sacrifice be equal to the offense committed?

2. How did God meet His own requirements for us?

G.  "Don't ever think that there are many ways to the divine. Jesus is the
    one qualified mediator, the only qualified candidate, and the only
    qualified Savior."
    1. Why is Jesus the only qualified mediator and Savior?

    2. How would you reply to someone who said Jesus is but one way
       to reach God?


*Discovering the Truth*

A.  Read Genesis 4:2–7, cf. Hebrews 11:4; Leviticus 10:1–3, cf. Leviticus
    16:1–5.
    1. Why did God refuse to accept Cain's sacrifice?

    2. Why did God judge Aaron's sons?

    3. Why does it matter how we approach God?

B.  Read Hebrews 7:24–28.
    1. How can Jesus hold a "permanent" priesthood (v. 24)?
    2. How is Jesus able to "save completely those who come to God
       through him" (v. 25)?

    3. How is Jesus described in verse 26? Why is this important?

    4. What is important about the phrase "once for all" in verse 27?

C.  Read Hebrews 10:11–14, 19–22.
    1. How many sacrifices did Jesus offer? What was the result of this
       offering?

2. How is it possible for someone who has been "made perfect forever" (past tense) at the same time said to be "being made holy" (present tense)?

3. How are we to approach God through Christ, according to verse 22? How is this made possible?

D. Read Job 9:32–35; 1 Timothy 2:5–6.
   1. What did Job crave? Why did he crave this?

   2. What have we been given in Christ, according to 1 Timothy? How were we given this gift?

E. Read John 14:6; Acts 4:10–12.
   1. What claim did Jesus make in John 14:6? How does His declaration disallow any other "road" to God?

   2. What claim did Peter make in Acts 4:10–12? How does his declaration disallow any other "road" to God?

## Lie 3:
### GOD IS MORE TOLERANT THAN HE USED TO BE

*Investigating the Lies*
A. "Is it safer for us to sin in this age than it was in the days of the Old Testament?"
   1. Answer this question.

   2. Why do you think some people believe it's "safer" to sin in this age than in Old Testament days?

B. Many people believe that "as we evolve to become more tolerant, our conception of God becomes more tolerant. Thus the New

Testament, with its emphasis on love, is a more mature, gracious representation of God."

1. How would you respond to someone who made a statement like this to you?

2. Why does the Old Testament major on "law" and the New Testament major on "grace"? Are the two mutually exclusive? Explain.

C. "The attributes of God revealed in the Old Testament are affirmed in the New. Even in the Old Testament we see the severity of God, but also His goodness; we see His strict judgments, but also His mercy."

1. List several attributes of God revealed in the Old Testament that are affirmed in the New Testament.

2. Describe several incidents from the Old Testament in which God's goodness and mercy are reported.

D. God is unchanging in at least three ways:
- His nature does not change
- His truth does not change
- His standards do not change

1. Show from the Bible that God's nature does not change.

2. Show from the Bible that God's truth does not change.

3. Show from the Bible that God's standards do not change.

4. What difference does it make to the way we behave, whether God changes or not?

E. "God's opinions have not changed; His penalties, if anything, are more severe. But there is a change in the timetable and method of punishment." Consider three ways in which God's administration of His world *does* change:
- From earthly to heavenly
- The old covenant versus. the new covenant
  a. God no longer deals with only one nation, but instead with individuals from all nations
  b. We are no longer to apply the death penalty for sin, but instead are to announce spiritual death for those who continue in sin
- Immediate, physical judgment versus. future, eternal judgment
  1. How has God's administration of His world changed from "earthly" to "heavenly"?

  2. Why does God now deal with individuals from all nations, rather than with a single nation? How did this change the way we are to deal with those who continue in sin?

  3. Why does God usually not bring immediate, physical judgment on those who continue to sin? How can we be sure there will ever be an accounting of sin?

F. Consider three principles regarding God's administration of His world:
- The greater the grace, the greater the judgment for refusing it
- We should never interpret the silence of God as the indifference of God
- Figuratively speaking, we must come to Sinai before we come to Zion
  1. In your own words, what do each of these principles mean?

2. Have you come to Sinai before coming to Zion? Explain.

*Discovering the Truth*

A.  Read Exodus 34:6–7; Psalms 90:2; Psalm 103:8–18.
    1. What do you learn about God in these passages?

    2. How do these truths about God affect you personally?

B.  Read James 1:17; Malachi 3:6; Hebrews 13:8.
    1. What do you learn about God in these passages?

    2. Why is it important to remember this truth?

C.  Read Isaiah 40:8; Psalm 119:89, 152.
    1. What do you learn about God's truth in these passages?

    2. How should this truth affect the way we live our lives?

D.  Read Hebrews 12:18–29.
    1. How is Mount Sinai described in verses 18–21? How is this significant?

    2. What six blessings of Mount Zion are described in verses 22–24?

    3. What warning is given in verse 25?

    4. How is this warning "given teeth" in verses 26–27?

    5. How does the author urge us to respond in verse 28?

    6. Why does the author end this passage with an emphasis on "consuming fire"?

E.  Read 1 Corinthians 5:9–12; 2 Peter 3:9.

1. How are believers to deal with professing Christians who continue
   in sin, according to 1 Corinthians 5? Why are not stronger
   measures to be applied?

2. What does 2 Peter 3:9 reveal about God's heart? How do we
   sometimes misunderstand His mercy?

F.  Read Hebrews 10:31; 2 Peter 3:10; Revelation 6:12–14; 20:13–15.

1. What do you learn about God in these passages?

2. How do these passages reveal an unchanging God?

G.  Compare Exodus 19:16–19 with Matthew 27:45–54.

1. What similarities do you find between these two passages? What
   differences?

2. What picture of God do you get from reading these passages
   together?

3. If you were to stand before God at this instant, do you think He
   would be pleased with you? Explain.

## Lie 4:

### GOD HAS NEVER PERSONALLY SUFFERED

*Investigating the Lies*

A.  "'A God who sees human suffering and fails to intervene is hardly
    worthy of worship.' What do you say to such a skeptic?"

1. Answer the question. What would *you* say?

2. Why do you think God fails to intervene to stop human suffering?

B. "We must forever do away with any notion of a weak God who is a victim of the chaos that has resulted from His original creation."
  1. How would you respond to someone who believed God really means well, but just doesn't have the power to stop pain and suffering?

  2. How do we know God is not "a victim of the chaos that has resulted from His original creation"?

C. "Our perpetual struggle is to reconcile God's love and the fact of human suffering. There are those who think that God has turned on them; He has abandoned them in their greatest hour of need."
  1. How do you reconcile God's love with the fact of human suffering?

  2. How would you try to minister to someone who thought God had turned on them, abandoned them?

D. "God is the silent sufferer; He knows, understands, and cares. He carries our sorrows close to His heart."
  1. Why is God a "silent" sufferer? What does this mean?

  2. How do we know that God "knows, understands, and cares"? How can we be sure that He "carries our sorrows close to His heart"?

E. "The clearest proof that God cares is found at the cross. Our comfort lies in the fact that our God not only walks with us, but also feels our sorrows and distresses."
  1. Why is the cross "the clearest proof that God cares"?

2. How does the cross help us in our sorrows and distresses today?

*Discovering the Truth*

A. Read Isaiah 49:13–16; Jeremiah 31:20; Hosea 11:8.

1. What is Zion's complaint in Isaiah 49:14? How does God respond in verse 15? What does this tell you about God's emotions?

2. What do you learn about God's emotions in Jeremiah 31:20? What sort of emotions does He have?

3. What do you learn about God's emotions in Hosea 11:8? Are they strong or weak? Explain.

B. Read Isaiah 43:1–4; Psalm 103:13–18.

1. What kind of picture does Isaiah paint of God? What comfort does this bring you?

2. What sort of compassion does God show toward us, according to Psalm 103? Why?

C. Read John 14:7–10.

1. What is the clearest way of knowing the Father, according to this passage?

2. What do you learn of God by observing Jesus?

D. Read Isaiah 53:3–10; Matthew 27:27–50.

1. How did Isaiah foresee the crucifixion of Christ? Name several specific prophecies. What do you learn here about the suffering of Christ?

2. How does Matthew's report of the Crucifixion fulfill Isaiah's prophecy? In what ways did Christ suffer?

E.  Read 2 Corinthians 5:19; 1 Peter 2:24.
1. Why did Christ go to the cross? Why did He suffer?

2. How do Christ's sufferings benefit us?

F.  Read Acts 20:28.
1. Why do you think Paul refers to the blood of God? Why not simply "the blood of Christ"?

2. What difference does it make to us whether God suffers?

Lie 5:

GOD IS OBLIGATED TO SAVE FOLLOWERS OF OTHER RELIGIONS

*Investigating the Lies*
A.  "Is it not hopelessly arrogant to suggest that there is one way to heaven and those who miss it through no fault of their own will be lost forever?"
1. How would you answer this question?

2. What do you believe happens to those who die without hearing of Christ?

B.  Consider three views suggested by some theologians for how non-Christians can be saved:
*   "Later light" view
*   God's foreknowledge view
*   God makes an exception view

1. Describe the reasoning behind each of these views.

2. Describe some problems with each of these views.

C. "The Scriptures require us to view other religions as the flawed attempts of man to reach God through human effort and insight."
   1. Where does the Bible give this teaching?

   2. How do other religions focus on the efforts of man to reach God? What is flawed with such efforts?

D. "God will not ask those who have never heard of Christ why they did not accept Him! That would be unjust. Judgment is always according to knowledge, according to the light given."
   1. How will God judge those who never heard of Christ?

   2. How much do you know of Christ? How have you responded to His claims? Explain.

E. "I believe those who are willing to admit that they fall short, those who turn from man-made gods and desire the one true God, are given additional light so that they can be led to the knowledge of Christ."
   1. On what basis can this statement be made?

   2. Do you agree with this statement? Explain.

F. "We can be sure that first there will be degrees of punishment commensurate with knowledge; and second that every bit of information about the circumstance and inner heart response will be taken into account."

1. Why can we be sure that there will be degrees of punishment commensurate with knowledge?

2. Why is it necessary to take into account someone's inner heart response?

G. "If God has a plan to save men and women without personal faith in Christ, He has not seen fit to reveal it. We must resist the temptation to make the Scriptures say what we think they should. Our role is to spread the gospel with the firm conviction that faith comes by hearing and people cannot believe what they do not know."

1. Why do you think God has left so many things unrevealed?

2. How are you fulfilling your role in spreading the gospel?

*Discovering the Truth*

A. Read John 14:6; Acts 4:12; 1 Timothy 2:5–6.
   1. What do each of these verses teach about how we can connect with God?

   2. How would the authors of these verses respond to the statement, "There are many ways to God"? Explain.

B. Read Deuteronomy 12:3; Psalm 96:5; 1 Corinthians 10:20–21.
   1. What do these verses teach about other "gods"?

   2. How were God's people to relate to these other gods?

C. Read Genesis 18:25; Romans 9:14–16.
   1. What do these verses assure us about God's judgment?

2. How can these verses give us peace of mind even when we don't have all the answers?

D. Read Romans 1:18–23; 2:12, 14–16.

1. How has God made plain to all mankind "his eternal power and divine nature"?

2. How will a person's conscience help to determine how that person is judged?

E. Read Acts 10; 11:14.

1. Retell the story of Cornelius in your own words.

2. Was Cornelius saved before or after Peter's visit (11:14)? Why is this important to note?

F. Read Acts 17:22–31.

1. What do you learn about God in this passage?

2. Did the apostle Paul believe the Athenians' gods were simply other pathways to the real God? Explain.

G. Read Luke 12:42–48.

1. What principle of divine judgment is expressed in this passage?

2. What is Jesus' challenge to all of us who hear this message?

H. Read Deuteronomy 29:29.

1. What kind of "secret things" do you believe this verse has in mind?

2. Why do you think God included this verse in the Bible?

## Lie 6:
### GOD TAKES NO RESPONSIBILITY FOR NATURAL DISASTERS

*Investigating the Lies*

A. "The immediate cause of a tornado is wind and temperature patterns, yet the ultimate cause of these events is God. He rules nature either directly or through secondary causes, but either way, He is in charge."

1. What is the difference between an "immediate," a "secondary," and an "ultimate" cause? What is significant about each?

2. How would you describe God's sovereign rule of the earth?

B. Consider three truths regarding natural disasters:
- The God who permits natural disasters could choose *not* to permit them
- God is sometimes pictured as being in control of nature, even without secondary causes
- If the heavens declare the glory of God, if it is true that the Lord reveals His attributes through the positive side of nature, why would not the calamities of nature also reveal something about His other attributes?

  1. In what way are natural disasters a "severe mercy"? How are such disasters intended to serve our good?

  2. What do the calamities of nature reveal about God's "other attributes"?

C. "Many people who do not believe that God controls the weather change their mind when a funnel cloud approaches them."

1. Why do you suppose such persons change their minds?

2. In what way is this statement similar to "There are no atheists in foxholes"?

D. "We should control nature to the best of our ability. God uses nature to both bless and challenge us; to feed and instruct us. God intends these forces, like the devil, for our eternal benefit that we might, so far as possible, overcome them."
   1. What is the difference between controlling nature and abusing it?

   2. How are we to benefit from overcoming nature?

E. To avoid charging God with evil, consider the following four observations:
   - God plays by a different set of rules
   - Final rewards and punishments are not meted out in this life
   - God does not delight in the suffering of humanity
   - As finite beings, we cannot judge an infinite being
     1. What set of rules does God "play by"? Why are these different from our own?

     2. Why are final rewards and punishments not meted out in this life?

     3. How do we know that God does not delight in the suffering of humanity?

     4. Why should finite beings refrain from judging an infinite being?

F. "Natural disasters are God's megaphone, shouting to us messages that we should be quick to learn:
   - Death is inevitable

- Judgment is coming
- We escape judgment by repentance"

1. Do these messages usually get through to the public when disaster strikes? Why or why not?

2. How does someone escape judgment by repentance? Have you so escaped? Explain.

G. "If nature is out of God's hands, then my life is also out of His hands."

1. Do you agree with this statement? Why or why not?

2. Do you believe your life is in God's hands? Explain.


*Discovering the Truth*

A. Read Genesis 3:16–19.

1. How did God respond to the sin of Adam and Eve? What happened?

2. How does this passage help to explain natural disasters?

B. Read Psalm 135:6–7; Genesis 6:17; Numbers 16:31–33.

1. What disasters are described here? Who caused them?

2. What are we to learn from these disasters?

C. Read Lamentations 3:38; Amos 3:6; Job 2:10.

1. In essence, what is each of these questions asking? What response do they expect?

2. How does it make you feel that God says He is ultimately responsible for the disasters that befall us? How does He want us to respond?

D. Read Luke 13:1–5.

1. What kind of response do you think the people expected from Jesus? Were they surprised by His answer? Explain.

2. What principle is Jesus teaching us in this passage? How are we to apply His teaching?

E. Read Romans 8:18–25.

1. Will our world always be in the wretched condition it now endures? Explain.

2. How are we to live in the time before our bodies and our world are redeemed (v. 25)? What are some practical ways to do this?

## Lie 7:

### GOD DOES NOT KNOW OUR DECISIONS BEFORE WE MAKE THEM

*Investigating the Lies*

A. "Today evangelical theologians are debating the question of whether God has exhaustive knowledge. Some insist that His knowledge is limited: He knows much more than we do, but He does not know our decisions until we make them."

1. Do you think this is an important debate? Why or why not?

2. Would it comfort you or alarm you to find out that God's knowledge was limited? Explain.

B. Consider two reasons why some theologians want to limit God's knowledge:
- They think this limitation is necessary to preserve human freedom
- They wish to protect God from the charge of ordaining evil

1. Why do these men think that limiting God's knowledge is the only way to preserve human freedom?

2. How would limiting God's knowledge protect Him from the charge of ordaining evil?

3. How do you personally respond to each of these conclusions? Why?

C. "Once God's knowledge is compromised, everything—but especially our confidence in Him—is jeopardized. In the end we shall see that God's exhaustive knowledge terrifies us, but thankfully, it is also a pillow on which we can rest our weary souls."
   1. Why does compromising God's knowledge jeopardize our trust in Him?

   2. In what way can we rest our weary souls on the pillow of God's omniscience? How is His infinite knowledge a comfort to us?

D. Consider four difficulties with the "openness of God" teaching:
   • It is contrary to Scripture
   • It jeopardizes the accuracy of prophecy
   • It erodes our confidence in the omnipotence of God
   • It undermines our trust in God
   1. What Bible passages refute the "openness of God"?

   2. How does this aberrant theology jeopardize the accuracy of prophecy?

   3. How does this aberrant theology erode our confidence in God's power?

   4. How does this aberrant theology undermine our trust in God?

5. How does belief in God's omniscience honor Scripture, uphold prophecy, encourage confidence in the omnipotence of God, and build our trust in God?

E. "Can you trust a God who does not know in the morning that you will be dead that evening? Does not the 'open view' of God make us feel sorry for Him, since He can only react as best He can to the unforeseen decisions of Satan and men?"
1. How would you answer the questions above?

2. What is your opinion of the "openness of God" theology? Why?

F. Psalm 139 teaches us at least three things about the exhaustive knowledge of God:
   • He knows us entirely
   • He knows us continually
   • He knows us prophetically
   1. How does God know us entirely?

   2. How does God know us continually?

   3. How does God know us prophetically?

   4. Does this exhaustive knowledge frighten you or comfort you? Explain.

*Discovering the Truth*
A. Read Isaiah 46:5–10; 41:21–24.
   1. How are false gods—idols—portrayed in these passages?

   2. How is the true God portrayed in these passages?

   3. What test does God suggest to prove which God is real?

B. Read Acts 4:27–28; 2:22–24.

   1. How do these passages portray the death of Christ? How certain was this event?

   2. How did this event depend on the foreknowledge and will of God?

C. Read Matthew 26:53–54.

   1. How did Jesus connect specific events of His life with biblical prophecies? How did these prophecies depend on God's foreknowledge?

   2. What is significant about the phrase, "must happen in this way"?

D. Read Luke 22:34, 54–62; John 13:19; John 6:64.

   1. How does Jesus' prophecy about Peter depend on God's foreknowledge?

   2. Why did Jesus tell His disciples about what was to happen (John 13:19)?

   3. How does Jesus' conviction about Judas depend on God's foreknowledge?

E. Read Genesis 6:6; 1 Samuel 15:11; 2 Samuel 24:16.

   1. Do these passages require that God did not foresee future events? Explain.

   2. How could God be "grieved" over something that happens, without wishing He had done something else?

F. Read Psalm 139.

   1. What do you learn about God's foreknowledge in this psalm?

2. Does this psalm inspire confidence in God or worry? Explain.

## Lie 8:

### THE FALL RUINED GOD'S PLAN

*Investigating the Lies*

A. "Here's how many people see it: God had Plan A, namely, that all of His created beings were to live in obedience and joy. But because these creatures took advantage of their free will, a percentage of the angels and later the entire human race were plunged into sin and its ugly consequences. In response, God initiated Plan B, entering the world in the person of Christ to redeem as many people as He could. Thankfully, we are invited to participate in this plan, and of course, we urge others to join us."

1. Have you heard some version of this scenario before? If so, where?

2. How do you react to this scenario? How do your friends react?

B. "Yes, there are terrifying evils in the world; God takes no delight in human suffering; and yet His eternal purposes are on track. Looked at from the standpoint of eternity, this is Plan A."

1. How can God's plan be on track even when evil exists, even when God loathes that evil?

2. How does the perspective of eternity radically affect the way God perceives the world?

C. "Creation turns out to be the first link in a chain of providential planning that will encompass all that God wanted to do. And the final link in the chain is always the glory of God."

1. List the main "links" in this chain. How are each necessary?

2. Why is the final link in the chain always the glory of God? Doesn't this make Him supremely vain?

D. "God has worked it so that our desires and His will converge with His purposes. The Bible does not see a contradiction between human responsibility and divine providence and direction."
   1. Describe an incident from your life where it eventually became clear that someone's poor or even evil choice nevertheless turned out to converge with God's purposes.

   2. How do you reconcile human responsibility with God's providence?

E. "We must distinguish between God's revealed will (which is not being done on earth) and His hidden will (or decree) that is always being carried out."
   1. Describe God's "revealed will." What is it?

   2. Describe God's "hidden will." What is it?

   3. How do the two work together to fulfill God's purposes?

F. "Only because God's sovereignty extends to every part of history can we be confident that each evil will be exchanged for some higher good."
   1. How does God's sovereignty give us this confidence?

   2. How does God's sovereignty make you feel? Explain.

G. "What if God wanted a company of people who would trust Him even though His ways are 'past finding out'? What if His desire was to have us believe that He is good, though there appears to be so much evidence to the contrary?"

1. How would you answer these two questions?

2. Why would God want such a company of people?

*Discovering the Truth*

A. Read Psalm 33:6; Revelation 4:11; Colossians 1:16.
   1. How did God create the universe, according to these texts?

   2. Did God make any mistakes in creation? Explain.

B. Read Job 42:2; Daniel 4:34–35; Ephesians 1:9–11.
   1. What do these verses tell us about God's will?

   2. How certain is God's vision for the future? Explain.

C. Read Isaiah 43:6–7; 60:21; Jeremiah 13:11; Psalm 106:8, 12; Romans 3:25, 26; 2 Thessalonians 1:9.
   1. What do you learn of God's glory in these verses?

   2. What is God's glory?

   3. Why is God's glory so important to Him?

D. Read Ephesians 1:4–6; 2 Timothy 1:8–9; Ephesians 3:9–11; Revelation 13:8.
   1. When did God choose us? Why is this significant?

   2. In what sense was Jesus "slain from the creation of the world"? How does this show that Calvary was always God's Plan A?

E. Read 1 Peter 1:6–8.
   1. How does suffering fit into God's plan for His people?

2. How does Peter instruct us to respond to suffering? Why?

Lie 9:

WE MUST CHOOSE BETWEEN GOD'S PLEASURES AND OUR OWN

*Investigating the Lies*

A. Many misinformed Christians believe they must either seek their own pleasures or give God pleasure by their obedience, but they cannot do both. "The choice is between personal happiness and duty, freedom or drudgery."

1. Why do you think many people feel this way? Have you ever felt this way? Explain.


2. Have you ever thought of God as a supremely happy God? Explain.


B. God himself has many pleasures, especially these three:
   - He delights in His Son
   - He delights in His creation
   - He delights in His people

   1. Why does God delight in His Son?


   2. Why does God delight in His creation?


   3. Why does God delight in His people?


   4. How can we find our delight in these three "pleasures"?


C. "We were created to seek pleasure. . . . Our problem is not that we seek happiness, but that we seek it in all the wrong places."

1. Do you agree that we were created to seek pleasure? Why or why not?

2. In what "wrong places" do we often seek our happiness? What dead ends have you personally experienced?

D. "Our temptation is to seek lesser pleasures . . . but lesser pleasures cannot deliver on their promises."
1. What is meant by "lesser pleasures"?

2. Why can't these "lesser pleasures" deliver on their promises?

E. "Spiritual maturity is substituting the greater pleasures for the lesser. . . . God satisfies in a way that other pleasures cannot. He gives us that which is of highest value; He gives us Himself."
1. Why does it take spiritual maturity to substitute the greater pleasures for the lesser? If the pleasures are really greater, why don't many people want them?

2. How does God give us Himself? In what way is He of highest value?

F. "God's pleasures and our pleasures are in harmony. . . . Getting to know God does not mean the renunciation of joy, but rather the fulfillment of it."
1. How do God's pleasures and our pleasures get in harmony?

2. How much do you know of real, deep joy? Explain.


*Discovering the Truth*
A. Read Psalm 115:3.
1. What determines the things God chooses to do?

2. How is God able to accomplish this?

3. Why does this assure us that God is supremely happy?

B. Read Matthew 17:5; Isaiah 42:1; Colossians 1:19.
   1. According to these verses, in what does God take pleasure?

   2. What is it here that brings Him pleasure?

   3. How can we find pleasure in the same thing?

C. Read Genesis 1:31; Psalm 104:31.
   1. According to these verses, in what does God take pleasure?

   2. What is it here that brings Him pleasure?

   3. How can we find pleasure in the same thing, without resorting to idolatry?

D. Read Psalm 23:3; Zephaniah 3:17.
   1. According to these verses, in what does God take pleasure?

   2. What is it here that brings Him pleasure?

   3. How can we find pleasure in the same thing?

E. Read Genesis 3:6.
   1. What "lesser pleasure" is described here?

   2. How did it deceive Adam and Eve into forsaking a greater pleasure?

   3. What can we learn from their experience?

F. Read Hebrews 11:24–26; 12:2; 1 John 2:17.
   1. What lesser pleasures tempted Moses? What lesser pleasures

tempted Jesus? What lesser pleasures tempt those who want to do the will of God?

2. How did Moses triumph over this temptation? How did Jesus? How can the one who wants to do the will of God?

G. Read 1 Peter 1:8–9; Psalms 16:5–11; 34:8-11; 37:4
   1. What kind of pleasures are to be found in God?

   2. How does one experience these pleasures?

   3. For how long will these pleasures last?

## Lie 10:
### GOD HELPS THOSE WHO HELP THEMSELVES

*Investigating the Lies*
A. "According to George Barna, about 75 percent of Americans believe the statement 'God helps those who help themselves' is right out of the Bible."
   1. Have you ever heard someone quote this "verse" as if it were out of the Bible? If so, describe what happened.

   2. Why do you think so many Americans believe this statement is biblical?

B. "God helps those who *cannot* help themselves. In fact, if He didn't help those who cannot help themselves, we would all be lost."
   1. Why does God help only those who *cannot* help themselves?

   2. Why would we all be lost if God did not help us?

C. *"Present, but not voting!* That's what we are, spiritually speaking, without the intervention of Christ. Those who are dead might be very alive physically; they can go to an opera, earn money, and ski in Colorado. Yes, we can do all those things and a whole lot more besides; but spiritually, without Christ we are dead, that is, disconnected from God."

1. How would you describe spiritual death to an unchurched person?

2. What does it mean to be "disconnected from God"? How does this play itself out in everyday life?

D. "It is not more difficult for God to save 'big' sinners than to save 'lesser' ones. Dead is dead, and resurrection is resurrection. You might think that your sin is too great, your past too sordid. But there is more grace in God's heart than there is sin in your past. The issue is not the greatness of your sin, but the application of God's powerful remedy."

1. Why isn't it more difficult for God to save "big" sinners than "lesser" ones? In God's eyes, are there "big" and "little" sinners? Explain.

2. Have you asked God to save you from your sins? If so, describe what happened. If not, why not?

E. "When God rescued us, He got what He wanted, namely, glory; we get what we want, namely His kindness."

1. What kind of "glory" did God get in rescuing us? Why did He want this "glory"?

2. What kind of "kindness" did God show us in rescuing us? How does this kindness continue today?

F.  God's grace is difficult to accept for two kinds of people:
    *   Those who are awash with guilt—they think, *God is so mad at me, there is no way He would accept me*
    *   Those who simmer in self-righteousness—they are offended by God's grace and consider it an insult to their sense of accomplishment
        1. How would you present the gospel to both kinds of people described here?

        2. Did you find it difficult to accept God's grace? Explain.


*Discovering the Truth*

A.  Read Ephesians 2:1–3; 2 Corinthians 4:4.
    1. What does it mean to be spiritually dead? What results from this death?

    2. What does it mean to be spiritually blind? What results from this blindness?

    3. In what condition are you? Explain.

B.  Read Romans 4:4–8; 11:5–6
    1. Why can't we work our way to God?

    2. Why can't we combine our work and God's grace to get to heaven?

C.  Read Ephesians 2:4–6.
    1. How did God intervene for us?

    2. Why did God intervene for us?

3. What did God's intervention for us accomplish?

D. Read 1 Corinthians 1:21; Romans 10:13–15.
1. What method does God use to bring us to Himself?

2. Why does this seem foolish to outsiders?

3. Why do you think God chose this method?

E. Read 2 Corinthians 5:17.
1. What happens to someone who accepts God's grace?

2. How is this to change all of life? In what ways does life change?

F. Read Titus 2:11–14.
1. To whom has the grace of God appeared? Why?

2. What does this grace teach us?

3. What does the return of Christ have to do with our current behavior?

4. How does this passage answer the statement "If I accept Christ and all my sins are forgiven, I can live however I want to"?